AF491624

CHRISTIAN BIBLE DRAMA SERIES
Christmas Edition

BELIEVE ME,

"FROM MIRACLE TO MIRACLE AND
FROM THE FIRST NIGHT TO EVERLASTING LIGHT"

I BELIEVE...

A Christmas pageant written in two acts depicting the mental struggles which people experienced trying to accept the miraculous acts of God as being real and true.

A presentation with music, drama, poetry and dance all interwoven into one continuous narrative

REV. DR. ERROL E. LESLIE

Copyright © 2024 **Errol Leslie Publishing**

All rights reserved. No part of this publication may be reproduced, distributed, or transmitted in any form or by any means, including photocopying, recording, or other electronic or mechanical methods, without the prior written permission of the publisher, except in the case of brief quotations embodied in critical reviews and certain other noncommercial uses permitted by copyright law. For permission requests, write to the publisher, addressed "Attention: Book Rights and Permission," at the address below.

Published in the United States of America

ISBN 979-8-89395-884-3 (SC)

Errol Leslie Publishing
222 West 6th Street
Suite 400, San Pedro, CA, 90731
errollesliepublishing@gmail.com
321 614 1546

Order Information and Rights Permission:

Quantity sales. Special discounts might be available on quantity purchases by corporations, associations, and others. For details, contact the publisher at the address above.

For Book Rights Adaptation and other Rights Permission.
Call us at toll-free 1-888-945-8513 or send us an email at
admin@stellarliterary.com.

I was blessed to be part of a theatrical production many years ago that brought together young people for an ecumenical ministry in the arts. I made lifelong friends, found a place to belong, and explored the limits, as well as leanings of my creative gifts. It was as a result of the lifelong creative foresight, insight, and genius of the Rev. Dr. Errol Leslie to whom I am forever indebted for the opportunity to play the character Lois. I reflect with fondness on the richness of the experience; it will always be held up as one of the best times in my youth when my skills and mind as a young person were affirmed and encouraged. We thank God for Rev. Leslie and trust that his example will be a template for youth ministry leaders.

—Candice Walker
Attorney-at-law, Kingston, Jamaica

This magnificent production brought to life an energetic reality of the Christmas story. Being a part of it was not only an honor, but the memory and excitement has left an indelible mark on all of us. As a very young pastor at the time, Rev. Leslie outdid himself by scripting, directing, and overseeing a successful play that left the audience very inspired.

—Nigel Reynolds
Dallas, Texas

It was an honor to have played Mary during the inaugural production in 1985. The memories of the energy, pride, and excitement still linger on. Our writer, director, producer, Rev. Leslie, masterfully combined his roles to ensure we delivered at every performance.

—Melissa Gooden-Bowleg
Nassau, Bahamas

I was thrilled to perform as Mary in one of Reverend Leslie's well-received, Christian theatrical productions.

—Simone Clarke
Florida, USA

Review from Explora books

Synopsis:

"Christian Bible Drama Series, Christmas Edition" takes readers on an extraordinary journey, diving deep into the untold emotions and unexplored details of the beloved Christmas narrative. Weaving together poetry, drama, music, and dance, the book breathes new life into the characters and events of that transformative season. It delves into the doubts, conflicts, and human experiences that surrounded the birth of Jesus, capturing the hearts and imaginations of readers.

The musical creates a visually captivating and emotionally resonant adaptation that will engage and inspire audiences worldwide. It holds immense potential to captivate audiences and leave a lasting impact. It will transport viewers into the vibrant scenes, immerse them in the characters' emotions, and allow them to experience the Christmas story in a profoundly personal way. The added visual and auditory elements will deepen the connection between the audience and the narrative, making it a truly transformative and memorable experience.

Highlights:

The musical has emotional depth as it brings to life the raw human emotions and conflicts faced by characters like Joseph and Mary, offering a fresh and relatable perspective on their journey. Audiences will witness their doubts, struggles, and unwavering faith, forging a profound connection with the story.

Imaginative retelling: It incorporates imaginative scenes and interwoven elements which breathes new life into the Christmas story, offering a unique and captivating take on its timeless themes. This creative approach will engage audiences and spark their curiosity, inviting them to reflect on the narrative in fresh and thought-provoking ways.

EXPLORA BOOKS, BOOK REVIEW -TWO:

"Christian Bible Drama Series, Christmas Edition" is an exceptional literary work that beautifully reimagines the timeless tale of the Christmas narrative. Pastor Leslie's revised edition takes readers on a captivating journey, exploring the untold emotions, conflicts, and intricate details surrounding the birth of Jesus. Through a masterful blend of poetry, drama, music, and dance, the author breathes new life into familiar characters and events, leaving readers spellbound.

What sets this book apart is its ability to evoke a deep sense of empathy and connection with the characters. Pastor Leslie artfully delves into the inner thoughts and struggles of figures like Joseph and Mary, inviting readers to experience their doubts, fears, and unwavering faith. By peeling back the layers of these characters' humanity, the author unveils a profound and relatable narrative that resonates with readers on a personal level.

The imaginative retelling of the Christmas story is nothing short of captivating. The inclusion of imaginative scenes and interwoven elements adds richness and depth to the familiar plot, sparking curiosity and challenging readers to contemplate the untold aspects of this transformative season. The author's vivid descriptions and meticulous attention to detail create a vivid tapestry that transports readers to the heart of biblical times.

Rating: ★★★★★ (5/5)

"Christian Bible Drama Series, Christmas Edition" is a literary masterpiece that deserves the highest praise. Pastor Leslie's work is a testament to the enduring power of storytelling, and this book is a must-read for anyone seeking a fresh and evocative retelling of the Christmas story.

"Christian Bible Drama Series, Christmas Edition," will touch the hearts of audiences, igniting a renewed sense of faith and hope. By staying true to the underlying theme of evangelism, the adaptation will encourage viewers to believe in Jesus and embrace the transformative power of His love.

BOOK TO FILM REVIEW

"The Christmas Journey" is a spectacular and emotionally resonant cinematic adaptation of the book "Christian Bible Drama Series, Christmas Edition (Revised Edition)." This captivating film brings to life the untold details and deep emotions surrounding the Christmas story, offering a fresh and visually stunning perspective on this beloved narrative.

Set in the ancient world, "The Christmas Journey" takes audiences on a breathtaking and immersive adventure through the lives of Joseph, Mary, and the other key characters of the Christmas narrative. The film explores the doubts, challenges, and profound faith that shaped their journey, while also delving into the societal pressures, gossip, and rumors that surrounded them.

Through meticulous attention to historical accuracy and awe-inspiring visual effects, "The Christmas Journey" transports viewers to the bustling streets of Bethlehem, the majestic halls of Herod's palace, and the serene beauty of the Judean countryside. The film's stunning cinematography and intricate set designs create a visually mesmerizing experience that truly brings the ancient world to life.

At the heart of "The Christmas Journey" are its powerful musical numbers. From soul-stirring solos to breathtaking ensemble performances, the film's original songs and choreography elevate the storytelling to new heights. Each musical moment serves as a window into the characters' innermost thoughts and emotions, allowing the audience to connect deeply with their journey and experiences.

As the story unfolds, "The Christmas Journey" emphasizes the universal themes of love, hope, and redemption. It showcases the transformative power of faith and the profound impact that a single act of obedience can have on the world. Through its engaging narrative and heartfelt performances, the film invites viewers to reflect on the true meaning of Christmas and the enduring message of peace and goodwill.

"The Christmas Journey" is a cinematic experience that will captivate audiences of all ages, believers and non-believers alike. It celebrates the beauty of the Christmas story while offering a fresh perspective that resonates with modern audiences. This visually stunning and emotionally resonant film is destined to become a beloved holiday classic, reminding us all of the power of faith, love, and the Christmas spirit.

[Following is an official OnlineBookClub.org review of "Christian Bible Drama Series -" by Rev Dr. Errol E. Leslie.] *5 out of 5 stars*

Rev. Dr. Errol E. Leslie creates two storylines that portray the events leading up to the birth of the Lord Jesus Christ in his book, ***Christian Bible Drama Series, Christmas Edition.*** This book is a collection of two dramas with the same message: the birth of Jesus Christ. Despite the differences in the storylines of both stories, certain key characters and events remain constant, such as the villainous character of King Herod and the saving power of God.

The stories involve the divine conception of a poor young girl, Mary, who was, at the time, betrothed to a young carpenter named Joseph. She gets that this may affect her engagement with him, but with the help of an angel, Joseph still takes her as his wife. When they eventually give birth to the child, King Herod does everything within his power to see that the ancient prophecy about the child does not come to pass.

Leslie uses this book to teach about the origin of Christmas and the importance of the celebration of Christmas in the Christian faith. The book has a touch of humor. For example, in the first story, despite the depletion of gold in Herod's country, the three wise men he sent to visit baby Jesus took gold to give him as one of the presents.

There are certain positive aspects of the book. First, the book is written in a simple and understandable language. Second, the author uses the book to teach certain lessons to Christians. For example, the author taught that God will not allow a person to be in a situation that the person cannot handle. This is exemplified in the story involving Mary when she was afraid of how Joseph would react to the news of her pregnancy. The book also teaches that God will certainly do everything to guide His own. Despite King Herod's decree for the killing of male children under the age of two, God still saved baby Jesus. Another positive aspect of the book is that it contains songs that can be sung independently during Christmas, and the author also provides the sol-fa notations of some songs.

I only found one error in the book. This shows that the book was professionally edited. Added to the positives identified above, I will be giving the book five out of five stars. The negative aspect I found was insufficient to deduct a star from my rating. I recommend this book to all Christians, especially those interested in Christmas dramas.

Contents

Foreword

When I was in seventh or eighth grade at school, I happened to have gone past the room which was used then as the school's auditorium following school one evening. In that room, there was a group of older students who were rehearsing what turned out to be a play. I was so intrigued by what was going on that I watched the proceedings from outside for about half an hour. Sometime on the following day, I inquired and sought some specifics as to what was really happening, and I was told that it was the school's drama group preparing for the annual secondary school's drama festival. I then asked if I could be a part of the group and was told that I was late for that year, but I could try for the following year. Interestingly, I also noticed that there was at least one student in the group who was younger than I was, so I felt kind of jealous.

I realized that I had had a natural passion for drama as I basically counted down the days for the next season and enthusiastically attended the first audition for parts to be given out for the play which was going to be done that following year. I was not totally disappointed because I was given a part as an understudy for one character. From that time forth, I was a part of the school's drama group and participated in every major production until I graduated. I enjoyed it immensely, and before I knew it, I was playing major star roles in my high school's drama productions.

For this introduction to theater, I recognize and pay tribute to my late high school vice principal who eventually became principal, Mr. Gordon Mead. While he is no longer with us, I would also acknowledge that his son, Andrew, remains in touch with his schoolmates through Facebook. Andrew was a very talented actor and, I might add, a natural comedian. God bless you, Andrew.

I also remember Mr. Roderick Ebanks and Ms. Karen Traynor as theater/drama teachers. While I do not know the life status of the latter two, I will note that they were both very supportive and helped to develop my early interest.

As far as schoolmates are concerned, I also acknowledge and recognize Mr. Basil Dawkins who eventually became a professional playwright and producer. I remember inviting Basil to attend a live performance of one of these musicals in 1989. He and I and a few other persons were engaged in an informal chit-chat following the production. In giving his feedback on the play, he said "This is one of the best Christmas plays that I have ever seen, and I have seen many." Basil, those words still resonate, and thirty-six years later, I still feel encouraged by those comments.

I also acknowledge the immediate former administrator general of Jamaica, Ms. Lona Brown. She was not only my classmate, but we co-starred in several high school productions in the early seventies. I remember very well seeing her perform in that first play which rehearsal I watched and was also moved by and impressed with her theater skills.

In twelfth grade (sixth form), as I battled with Shakespeare, Lord Byron, Chaucer, Jane Austen, Aldous Huxley, et al., in English Literature, I was again fortunate to have the above-mentioned Mrs. Lona Brown, as well as Mr. Glenroy Mellish, Mr. Henry Wright, and several others as my classmates sitting at the feet of Mr. Watts learning how to analyze poems, plays, and other pieces of literature. Some fundamentals about writing would have stuck with me from my interaction with those classmates and teachers.

Once I graduated high school, I taught as a pretrained teacher at a secondary school. I immediately started a drama and music club, and in the one year I was there, I was able to get the students to put on an original play which I had written for a concert and which also included some music and singing. I continued pursuing my innate passion for the arts when I entered seminary at the United Theological College of the West Indies, and for four years, I was part of both the drama group as well as the UTCWI Singers.

There was a parallel situation developing while I explored music and drama at the levels mentioned. I was also leader for my church's youth group, and I was constantly writing, directing, and producing short plays. Several of these plays were done at a competitive level while others were just done causally in church but would always carry a message. Several of the short plays which I wrote then were performed in a few neighboring churches.

In the year 1985, I began writing my second Christmas musical: BELIEVE ME, I BELIEVE as a sequel to my first which was written in 1982. This one took on a different slant in terms of plot, but it gave me the ability to create a second set of imaginary scenarios while still maintaining the basic message of the Christmas story. As was the case with the 1982 production, the young people across the circuit embraced this second musical and performed it several times in Central Jamaica. After those performances, I again turned my attention to publishing, but once more, that did not happen. I had also begun to develop plots in my head, which would have been associated with several Bible stories and/or characters, but I did not follow through on completing them.

When I was transferred to the Savlamar Circuit of Methodist Churches in 1986, there was still one last opportunity for me to have This second musical performed. The year was 1989, and this time, I reached out to the young people in many churches in the town—Methodist and non-Methodist alike. What a great time of fellowship and sharing we had as we also had several performances of **BELIEVE ME, I BELIEVE** across several neighboring towns in Western Jamaica. It was at the very last performance done in the auditorium of my alma mater Manning's School that I heard those encouraging words from the playwright, producer, and former schoolmate, Mr. Basil Dawkins whose works were well-known regionally across the Caribbean.

I think that there is some significance in the fact that I was first introduced to theater productions at the auditorium for my high school, and now I had this last major performance of my second Christmas musical at the same venue.

Finally, after almost forty years since they were written, I offer this Christmas musical to the world. I trust that it will be found to be uplifting and the intended message of Christmas will resonate with persons across the world.

More importantly, I pray that lives will be changed spiritually and for the better as a result of whether watching these productions being done or participating in them in one way or the other.

Preface

This Christmas musical can be used in any one of several ways. It can be used in it's entirety as a full-length production or specific scenes can be extracted from it and shared as shorter plays. Depending on the setting, there are instances where the music or songs may be omitted although doing so may take away from the flow of the plot. As such, I would encourage directors to include the music and the dance, as these combinations certainly do add to the effect of the message. Directors may have a part of the cast sing the group songs, but it might be just as or even more effective if there was a separate choir and maybe orchestra preparing and singing the group musical pieces at the appropriate time. Where appropriate, the original songs may even be recited as poems in certain settings. This musical was originally written for youth and young adults to share in during the season of advent.

However, if there is an opportunity for more senior adults to participate, they would be welcomed to do so. Where appropriate, players are encouraged to direct some statements to the audience since the hope is that the Christmas message would resonate again with persons in the audience.

Thank you for your interest in this Christmas musical and with your prayers and God's help, I trust that there will be several more musicals flowing from my pen which would be centered around biblical stories and plots. This one is from the Christmas edition, but hopefully, there will be more to come.

Hence the general title of this series, ***Christian Drama Bible Series.***

BELIEVE ME, I BELIEVE...

A Christmas pageant written in two acts depicting the mental struggles which people experienced trying to accept the miraculous acts of God as being real and true.

Written by: Errol E. Leslie

Characters:

Mary: A young lady
Joseph: her fiancé
Elizabeth: Mary's cousin
Zacharias: Elizabeth's husband
Charlotte: Mary's parents
Ephariam
Rhoda: Joseph's parents
Jepheth
Shamna: Elizabeth's brother
Rebecca: his (Shamna's) wife
Simeon: An old man of God
Lois: worker at the inn
Sim: worker at the inn

Tod: worker at the inn
Japhat: keeper of the stable
Herod: the king
Priscilla: his wife
Reuben: the prince
Leah: the princess
Josiah: chief attendant to King Herod.
Ben and Rachel: couple wanting to stay at inn
Two attendants
Four Shepherds (Nashon, Hezron, Jotham, Zadok)
Wise Men
Singers
Dancers

Readers Prologue

Stage is lit. Curtain opens on narrator after one verse of prerecorded version of "Once in Royal David's City" is played or sung live by choir or soloist. Music softens into background as narrator recites first verses. The company gradually comes on stage four at a time, curiously and inquiringly until the end of the fourth verse by which time the whole company is present and join in the singing of the fifth verse and sixth.

Once in royal David's city,
Stood lowly cattle shed,
Where a mother laid her baby
In a manger for His bed:
Mary was that mother mild,
Jesus Christ her little child.

*

He came down to earth from heaven,
Who is God and Lord of all,
And His shelter was a stable,
And His cradle was a stall;
With the poor and meek and lowly,
Lived on earth our Savior holy.

*

And through all
His wondrous childhood,
He would honor and obey,
Love and watch the lowly mother,
In whose gentle arms He lay.
Christian children all should be,
Mild, obedient, good as He.

*

For He is our childhood's pattern,
Day by day like us He grew,
He was little, weak, and helpless,
Tears and smiles like us He knew,
And He feeleth for our sadness,
And He shareth in our gladness.

*

And our eyes at last shall see Him,
Through His own redeeming love;
For that child so dear and gentle,
Is our Lord in heaven above,
And He leads His children on,
To the place where He is gone.

*

Not in that poor lowly stable,
With the oxen standing by,
We shall see Him, but in heaven,
Set at God's right hand on high;
When like stars
His children crowned,
All in white shall be around.

VERSE/CHORAL SPEAKING:
THE COMPANY

The Lord Jesus Came

Yes, this is what we're here to tell
That Glorious news you'll love so well
In song and drama, verse, and dance
So everyone will have a chance
To hear that tale of worldwide fame
Which simply says "The Lord Jesus Came"

FIRST SPEAKER	Shall we hear the tale?
SECOND SPEAKER	We shall hear the tale!
GROUP	It's worth hearing the tale!
FIRST SPEAKER	Then listen you who have ears to hear
SECOND SPEAKER	All eyes open if you really care
GROUP	The tale speaks of that famous name telling us "The Lord Jesus Came"

Now Joseph and Mary were never well known
Zacharias and Elizabeth were not from the town.
But all these four had one common touch
And within a short while they learnt so much
The Lord would use them to achieve great things
To see to the welfare of the king of kings
For 'twas into the household of two of these same
That Him of which we speak, The Lord Jesus Came.
Old Herod was angry that the Lord Jesus Came
For with the Lord's coming, his throne became lame
So astrologers and wise men he sent on their beasts
To pursue a star which stood in the east
He killed and he killed but he still missed his mark
So Mary and Joseph remained happy as a lark
For the Lord Jesus came and brought all the glory
And now we can talk about the Christmas story…
The Christmas story. The Christmas story,
THE CHRISTMAS STORY!

(Group join in singing "The Christmas Story")

We want to tell you 'bout the Christmas Story
Tell you how the angel came from glory
How he came to the priest and the maiden
They were called Zacharias and Mary
Then next he went to Joseph
And convinced him to father the baby
Even the shepherds in the fields
Their lives to God did yield
And left the sheep with no shield.

CHO
The story is about the Lord Jesus Christ; He's
the baby that was born
In a manger dark and dirty that first Christmas
morn
He came into the world, To make us clean and
feel forever worthy
For now in our lives, we have Jesus Christ

We give thanks to God, we rejoice and are glad
That the Father sent Him to save us
So lift up your hands, give thanks to our heavenly
Dad

Tell everybody 'bout the Christmas story
For It has a lasting place in history
We must tell it to the aged and the children
Till it sticks with the wayward and heathen
We'll keep this message flowing
Anywhere that we may still be going
Go tell your neighbors and your friends
The world from end to end.
His son The Father did send.

(Group dance follows; appropriate version of "Deck the Halls")
(Lights glow dim as Zacharias appears backstage. He is working at the altar. The group appears front stage—half crouching.)

GROUP

Now be quiet for the action
And give your full attention
As all mankind seeks
The Lord God speaks
To one well stricken in years
And who shed plenty of tears
For no one came from his seed
So he might even feed
A son or grandson or whatever of his line
Oh No! Oh No! He saw not a sign
So they held him in prayer, O so sincere
To everyone, he was so dear
All who knew him showed their care
Since his wife Elizabeth, no child did bear

Zacharias	They're talking about me. Yes. I am Zachariahs; the old man. Want to know my age? Guess you'd love to. Very old I can tell you, all my youth is gone. There is no more hope for all my days are nearly done. Why has this happened to me? *(in anguish)* Oh Lord, why me? Why have I been afflicted? *(Continues to mime prayer while group picks up story.)*
GROUP	*(kneeling and in prayerful mood)* And so, he prayed and prayed and prayed. Until up on the altar he stretched out and laid his hands by his side as though he were dead. So all kinds of thoughts must have gone through his head. The lord gently prepared him for the shock of his life, A son would be born to his age-stricken wife.

(Dance group comes in to appropriate piece of Christmas music with fast/upbeat tempo)

(Group leaves. Figure representing angel appears on stage. Light shines from figure onto Zacharias...by now he is dreaming.)

Angel Voice	Zacharias! *(louder)* Zacharias! *(Lights flash as angel speaks)*
Zach	*(jumping up and starting to run)* Oh my God, what is this?
Angel Voice	Be calm, my friend, and have no fear. The voice you hear is that of the Lord.
Zach	But… But… Where do you come from? What do you want?
Angel Voice	The Lord God has sent me to let you know that your prayers have been heard.
Zach	Prayers! What prayers! *(Now fully awake as light brightens)*

Angel Voice	Your prayers. You prayed and asked that the Lord would give you a child. The Lord will grant your wish. Your wife Elizabeth will bear you a son and you shall call his name John.
Zach	Away from me, you evil spirit, and go back to satan from which you came. You know not what…
Angel Voice	It is the truth. I have come from God, trust Jehovah, believe his word. This boy shall bring you joy and gladness for many shall rejoice at his birth. He shall be great in the sight of the Lord, and he shall drink no wine or strong drink.
Zach	I think I recall the words of scripture "He… He shall separate Himself from wine and strong drink and shall drink no vinegar of wine or vinegar of strong drink, neither shall he drink any liquor of grapes or dried. Now therefore beware, I pray thee, and drink not wine nor strong drink and eat not any unclean thing for lo thou shalt conceive and bear a son and no razor shall come on his head; For the child shall begin to deliver Israel out of the hand of the Philistine."
Angel Voice	He shall be filled with the Holy Ghost even from his mother's womb. Many of the children of Israel shall he turn unto the Lord their God. And he shall go before his face in the spirit and power of Elijah to turn the hearts of the fathers to the children.
Group	*A man of God came unto me and his countenance was like the countenance of an angel of God, very terrible, but I asked not whence he was; neither told me his name. Behold I shall send my messenger and he shall prepare the way before me and the Lord whom you seek shall suddenly come to his temple even the messenger of the covenant whom ye delight in: behold he shall come, saith the Lord of hosts.*

Angel Voice	He shall cause the disobedient to walk in the wisdom of the just to make ready for the Lord a people prepared for him.
Zach	It is hard to believe this. I am such an old man and my wife is well stricken in years. Could this really be true? No! It is not.
Angel Voice	Yes, it is true. I am Gabriel, the angel of God. You need to believe me. Because you have not believed, you will not be able to speak until all those things come to pass. As soon as I leave, you will be struck dumb. Is there any last word that you would have to say?
Zach Sings	Don't Leave Me, Guardian Angel Don't leave me, guardian angel What more is there to tell? Stay right here close beside me If I will a father be I do not want for you to grieve. Believe me, I believe! Don't leave me, Guardian angel Shall I go ring my bell? To tell the world the great news That I hope they won't refuse This news I want them to receive Believe me, I Believe! Don't leave me, Guardian angel I love this news so well It gives me joy and gladness Even though I failed the test Don't punish me as God did Eve Believe me, I believe! Don't leave me, guardian angel Or I might go to hell I want my voice forever

So never leave me, never
My life my word to God I give
Believe me, I believe.
(Focus goes back to chorus front stage)

Group   Meanwhile the people outside of the temple
wondered about Zacharias.

First Speaker   Where is Zacharias?

Second Speaker   What's taking him so long?

Third Speaker   Where could he really be?

Group   I think about that old man
For whom I pray a lot
I think about the Lord's plan
And wonder what he's got
An angel told him something
Is he to be a king?

*(The angel departs. Zach comes front stage showing
signs of being dumb.)*

(Company sings good news bad news)

Good news! Bad news! What's the news?
You godly folk must be confused.
One man gets a son but is struck dumb
Good news for others but bad for some.

Speak low, speak high! Tell me why
Your voice is gone back to the sky
And the splendid news now seems quite bad.
This news will cause you to feel so sad

Some lose, some gain what's the pain
The Lord will give you back again
You may not know how the lord will work
He will remove all the pain and irk.

Bad news now, but good's to come
Two will be born instead of one
You have to believe me when I say
There's going to be a brighter day
Bridge
Sing Gloria, Gloria, Gloria, Gloria
Glory to God in the highest
For he who's to come; the son of man
Oh glory, glory be!
Hallelujah Praise be to God
Glory to God! Glory to God
Glory to God in the highest!
(Curtain)

Act I, Scene I
Zacharias's Home

Zacharias is seated alone in a simple setting. He tries to read his scroll. There is soft Christmas music in the background. After a while, there is a rap on the door; it is Mary.

Mary	*(Entering)* Elizabeth! Elizabeth! *(She is excited; sees Zach)* Oh! Zacharias! *(Zach looks up; she lowers her voice.)* Zacharias! *(Zacharias gets up but can say nothing; he can only utter strange sounds.)* Zacharias, what is wrong with you? You won't speak to me. *(He makes signs to her)* Oh God, what is happening? *(Elizabeth enters)* Elizabeth! Oh, sweet Elizabeth.
Elizabeth	*(They move to embrace each other, patting each other and starting to cry. Elizabeth changes her tone of voice.)* Lord, I thank you! Lord, I thank you.
Mary	*(as they break their embrace)* Elizabeth, I am so exited! It is unbelievable. All that has happened…
Elizabeth	But you must be, my dear. So am I. Even more excited. To be a mother at my age…
Mary	Is it true? Do you really believe this?
Elizabeth	It is strange, my dear, very strange, but believe me! I believe. *(Mary shrugs somewhat)* Why don't we sit down and talk about it. There is so much to talk about really! *(Zacharias tries to say something as they move toward the seat.)*
Mary	What's wrong with Zacharias?
Elizabeth	He is only being punished for his unbelief. An angel told him…

Mary	An angel? An angel came to me!
Elizabeth	One visited Zacharias too. He told him that God had answered our prayers and that I was going to have a child. Of course, my dear husband found it hard to believe since he felt we were both too old. Because of this, he has lost his voice, and it will only return after the child is born.
Mary	Oh no! *(Zach tries to speak again and, on failing, decides to make signs)* What is he trying to say now?
Elizabeth	I'm not sure. I suppose he is trying to tell you a little more of the story of how it happened. It is a real agony. Mental agony that he must be going through now. But it won't be for a long time. Our child will be born soon.
Mary	Well, I couldn't believe it at first either. When the angel told me, I was going to have a child, I could not believe it. I still have not known a man. I may have lost my voice too.
Elizabeth	Good thing you didn't. The Lord God in his wisdom knows why certain things are allowed to happen.
Mary	Oh, praise be to God. *(Shamna and Rebecca enter. They are visiting Elizabeth.)* Who are these?
Elizabeth	Oh, I am sorry, Mary, I should have told you that Shamna and Rebecca are visiting with us. Let me introduce. Shamna…this is…
Shamna	No introductions, I know my little cousin Mary. She continues to be a pretty little girl.
Elizabeth	But poor Mary wouldn't remember you, dear. You left this town when she was barely able to recognize persons.
Shamna	Mary, I am your big cousin Shamna, I knew you when you were *(gesturing)* this tall. This is my wife, Rebecca. She is not used to talking much. Always a bit quiet and reserved.
Rebecca	Hi, dear, what a joy to see you.

Shamna	You're going to make someone a real pretty wife…and I hear you are to become a pretty mother soon. Which one will come first?
Elizabeth	Shamna. *(Zach tries to speak again)* Oh, Shamna could you sit inside with Zacharias for a while. There is going to be all ladies talk now.
Mary	Nice to see you, big cousin, real nice.
Shamna	Nice seeing you too, girl. Will be right back. *(Turns to take Zach toward door)*
Rebecca	He's in a talking mood today. You'll never stop him. *(Shamna turns back, having shoved Zach inside)*
Shamna	Not finished yet. Want to find out more about my little cousin.
Mary	Oh, he is one of those?
Elizabeth	Mary dear, won't you tell us what your plans are? You are so lucky. You're blessed among women.
Mary	Well, really, I don't know. There comes a time in your life when you know that something is happening to you. The more you know what it is happening, the harder it is to accept and to believe it.
Shamna	All right, so you are going to become a mother, so what? You know you make me so proud of you. *(Goes over to Mary)* You're going to be a mother… You're going to be a mother. *(Takes her by the shoulder)* You must believe, you must believe, do you believe now? Do…you…believe?
Mary	Let me see… Ah… Yes, believe me, I believe. God came to me. Yes, an angel came to me. *(She sings)*

"An Angel Came to See Me"

While I was sleeping in my bed
An angel came to me and said
   Mary, Mary, have no fear

You'll like the news you're going to hear
You're going to have a baby boy
And he will fill the world with joy
He'll save the people from their sin
For through their hearts, he'll enter in.

CHORUS

Call Him, Call him, call him Jesus
Call Him, call him Lord.

I was asleep, I was awake
I did not know what steps to take
Within my heart, I knew no man
I could not understand God's plan
How could I have a baby boy
So he could fill the world with joy
Yet while I thought it was a dream
The Lord said clearly, "Here's your theme"

The angel left and went His way
He left me dazed for many a day
I thought about what he had said
As I still lay inside my bed
I'm gonna have a baby boy
And he will fill the world with joy
He'll save the people from their sin
For through their hearts, he'll enter in.

Shamna	That's my little baby cousin All right…yeah! *(begins to applause)*
Rebecca	Shamna, you're overexcited. You need to show a little more reverence when we're dealing with God's plan. You must have the residue of overnight wine left inside you.

Shamna

Very well, then I shall take my leave… You ladies do not know how to appreciate good company. Cheerio, Mary, looking forward to seeing your little boy. *(Starts to leave then turns around)* By the way, what would you do if it turns out to be a little girl…ha…ha *(leaves)*

Rebecca

Good heavens, he is on form.

Elizabeth

I suppose it takes all forms to make up this world. Does it not? There would be no excitement if we didn't have a few like those.

Rebecca

Yet, my dear, enough is enough, Mary, you're not saying anything. Have you become speechless like Zacharias?

Mary

Not really, I'm just thinking.

Elizabeth

What about? Do you still not believe?

Mary

Of course. I can accept the truth; I can accept God's plan, but can the rest of the world accept? Will my parents be able to accept the truth? You know I was always held in high esteem. How can I convince them that I am still pure? *(She begins to get emotional)* I am a liar, I am a cheat, I am a traitor. I am a…everything… that's all you'll hear. The angel never appeared to everyone; he only appeared to me. *(Starts to cry)* I don't think this is fair to me you know. It should have happened to someone else. *(Screams at Elizabeth)* Elizabeth!

Elizabeth

(breaking down too) Do not look at it that way, Mary. God would never allow you to carry more than you can bear.

Mary

You wouldn't know the shame. You wouldn't know the disgrace! Can you imagine the talk of this town? *(sarcastically)* "Mary, the little straight-line girl, is pregnant and does not know who the father is."

Rebecca

Oh No! Please, Mary.

Mary	And then…and then…*(breaks down again)* There is Joseph.
Rebeca	Who?
Mary	Joseph! What can I tell him? How can I tell him?
Rebecca	But who is Joseph?
Mary	I am engaged to him. We were supposed to be getting married shortly…*(speaks to an imaginary Joseph)* Joseph! Guess what? I'm pregnant! That won't do. Joseph, if I tell you that I am pregnant, would you believe it? Won't do either. *(In ecstasy)* I must find a way out! I must.
Elizabeth	You will find a way out. It's not that hard. You need to learn to trust God. Have some faith, Mary. Do not allow the same thing to happen to you as it happened to Zacharias. Do you recall how many persons referred to in scriptures learnt that they were to put their trust in God? There is an omnipotent being behind this world. *(Begins to walk all over the stage building up a crescendo)* He sees and he knows. He cares and He understands. He loves us forever. This life ought to be one of the constant, hope, trust, and confidence, which we have in God. *(Goes front stage as if addressing audience)* Abraham lived by faith, hope, trust, confidence, and belief in God. And so must we. We must believe. Believe me, I believe. *(group comes on for dance "I Believe for Every Drop of Rain That Falls" or other appropriate song relating to faith and trust. As they leave stage, Mary continues.)*
Mary	Thank you, Elizabeth. I feel so much better now. I needed that kind of consolation really. After all, I am the Lord's chosen one to be the mother of the savior of the world.
Elizabeth	And really, for me to have the privilege of the mother of the Savior of the world come to me. It is an honor, a great honor! *(She hugs Mary.)*

Rebecca	I will not have a child, yet I share your joy. I am so happy to be a part of the family. *(There is a knock at the door. It is Joseph. He does not yet know what has happened.)* There is someone at the door, Elizabeth. Shall I go see who it is?
Elizabeth	Sure! Thank you. *(Rebecca moves toward door, and as she leaves…to Mary)* She is such a sweetheart. The best wife my brother could ever find.
Mary	I know, I can see it! *(Rebecca reenters)*
Rebecca	Mary…it is…it is… Are you expecting Joseph to visit here?
Mary and Elizabeth	Joseph?
Rebeca	An elegant gentleman, wearing a beard, and is quite pleasant?
Elizabeth	Let me go and see. *(She leaves)*
Mary	What am I going to tell him?
Rebecca	Just be calm. The Lord will tell him. Just remember all the words of consolation you just received.
Mary	*(holding her abdomen)* Hey, Joseph. Here is your son, how about that for greetings?
Rebecca	You still haven't learned to relax…here they come. *(Joseph and Elizabeth enter)*
Mary	Joseph *(goes across and embraces him)*, how did you know I was here?
Joseph	Oh, well I guess I did not find you at your mom nor by your uncle so I guess you have to be by big cousin. Elizabeth, I am smart. Can't you see?
Mary	Joseph, that was the easiest thing to work out. Oh, by the way, you need to meet Rebeca. She is married to Elizabeth's brother, Shamna. Rebeca, this is Joseph. We are due to be married shortly.
Rebecca	Hello, Joseph, I must say you are quite a charm.

Joseph	Well, thank you, Rebeca, it's good to meet you. You see my friend Mary is such a beauty, one really has to try to measure up to her. *(They all chuckle a little; to Mary)* Sweetheart, we are supposed to be going visiting this evening. I see your memory's slipping.
Mary	Goodness gracious, but you did not remind me. Is it too late? Or perhaps we could just spend the rest of the evening with Elizabeth. She could do well with our company. Isn't that so, Elizabeth?
Elizabeth	Sure, you know I could have you both all evening. You are extra special people.
Joseph	So where is the old boy, Zacharias? I guess he is still praying in the temple, eh? What a devout God-fearing man he is.
Elizabeth	Oh, resting, it has been so hectic for him over the past few days.
Joseph	Oh, I can just imagine, I know the old boy all right.
Elizabeth	You'll need to know the rest of the news. *(Rebeca and Mary glance at each other.)*
Joseph	News? What news? Is it good or bad?
Elizabeth	Both…no… Actually, it depends on you. *(Mary turns to leave the stage)* Mary, where are you going?
Mary	Just to see if Zacharias is awake really, I'm not worried.
Joseph	Worried? What is it really? Do, please, do not hold me in suspense, Mary.
Mary	Yes, dear. Would you like to guess?
Rebecca	Well, Joseph, what news could you hear that would make you the happiest?
Elizabeth	Or what news could you hear that might make you the saddest?
Joseph	Riddles, riddles, riddles.
Rebecca	Then guess the riddle.

Joseph	Patience, my patience; I do not have a lot. My patience is running out.
Mary	All right…ready? Hold your breath.
Joseph	*(chuckling)* I am holding it.
Mary	Joseph, Elizabeth, is going to have a baby and I am going to…
Joseph	Seriously now, ladies.
Elizabeth	She is serious, Joseph. I am with child. I swear to it.
Joseph	Elizabeth, you are ripe in age and Zacharias even more so.
Elizabeth	Not so. We are both ripe in age, but it just speaks of the miraculous power of our God. The angel Gabriel appeared to Zacharias and told him that we were going to have a child. As he prayed in the temple, the angel appeared to him, so he told me anyway.
Joseph	I remember Sarah of old. She conceived when she was past age, but I never thought that there would be another such.
Mary	Neither did I, but we have got to believe it, Joseph. If we don't, then let me tell you why Zacharias has been resting. He did not believe the angel; he did not seem able to accept God's miracle and so God decided to punish him for displaying unbelief. Now he will not be able to speak until the child is born.
Joseph	Oh no.
Rebecca	Oh yes. It is so. I am sure you would not want that to happen to you. Would you?
Joseph	Certainly not. Lord, I pray it does not happen to me. I must go to see Zacharias to see if this is really happening.
Elizabeth	No, Joseph. Let him still get rest. He needs to be by himself. He must be alone.
Joseph	I am curious. Oh, I am so anxious.

Elizabeth	Well, there is more to hear. How would you like to become a father yourself?
Joseph	Oh, I am looking forward to that. *(gesturing)* To hold my little boy in my arms? Mary, I can't wait.
Elizabeth	Well, you don't have a long time to wait for Mary is with child too.
Mary	Elizabeth! *(expressing shock the news has burst out)*
Rebecca	Mary!
Joseph	You have all gone crazy, what are you talking about?
Mary	Joseph, please listen to me. *(nervously)* You have got to believe every word I say. You must trust me. Do you hear me?
Joseph	Speak, Mary, I will hear you.
Mary	We're really to become parents soon. *(She holds her head down and then looks up, as he has not responded; they look at each other momentarily.)* Did you hear me, Joseph? We are going to have a son.
Joseph	We?
Mary	Yes, Joseph, you and I.
Joseph	Me? *(He looks at Mary and then at the others, they all look at each other)* You have had plenty of wine, Mary. You are drunk.
Mary	Am I? No, Joseph, I am not.
Rebecca	She is not. An angel appeared to her as well.
Joseph	An angel appeared to her? What angel?
Elizabeth	The angel Gabriel appeared to her.
Mary	An angel appeared to me.

(Sings the first verse of "An Angel Appeared")

An Angel Came to See Me

While I was sleeping in my bed
An angel came to me and said
Mary, Mary, have no fear

You'll like the news you're going to hear
You're going to have a baby boy
And he will fill the world with joy
He'll save the people from their sin
For through their hearts, he'll enter in.

CHORUS
Call Him, Call him, call him Jesus
Call Him, call him Lord.

*(Rebecca and Elizabeth join in with the added
verse, singing to Joseph as he sits and thinks.)*

You have your doubts you don't believe
And yet you will that child receive
Joseph, Joseph, hear God's word
And join us now in one accord.
You're going to have a baby boy
And he will fill the world with joy
He'll save the people from their sin
For through their hearts, he'll enter in.

CHORUS:
Call Him, Call him, call him Jesus
Call Him, call him Lord.

Joseph	*(going down on his knees)* Oh thou God who hast all power; thou God who dwellest in truth. The God of our fathers of Abraham, Isaac, and Jacob, look now upon your servant.
	(End of scene)

Act I, Scene II
The Home of Mary's Parents

Joseph is alone on stage as the lights brighten on him; he
is parading the stage

Joseph   I Am Alone

                   I am alone, there's none who walks beside me
                   My one true love has thrown me to the sea
                   I'm lost, I'm down, I'm everything that's wrong
                   A bachelor for life I'm meant to be
                   For why, the reason I just cannot know
                   I just put my trust in him who loves me so.

                   I am alone my mom and dad are gone
                   And here I stand and stare; Oh yes alone
                   The nerves, the lies, I take them with a smile
                   But what are smiles when anger inside burns
                   Like Job of old, I still believe in God
                   He knows I'm pure, and in his paths, I trod

                   I am alone, It's just my Lord who's with me
                   There's none who loves me half as much as he
                   But still; Oh yes, if that, dear Lord, is with me
                   I'm not alone, I fall yet I will rise
                   And so, oh God, once more I draw close to you
                   Just guide me, tell me what I ought to do.

*(Group sings "Precious Lord, Take My Hand" or other appropriate
song with the message of God carrying His people in His Hands. There is a
solitary dancer. Group leaves stage and Joseph is alone again. Mary enters.)*

Mary	You need to believe me, Joseph. You're not being fair to me. *(pause)* I do really love you. *(pause)* I'll die if you didn't marry me. *(pause)* (*Then she reaches over to touch him.*) Joseph.
Joseph	*(backing off)* Do not touch me, Mary.
Mary	Joseph, don't say that.
Joseph	Your hands are filthy.
Mary	They are not. You are hurting God, and you are going to be sorry.
Joseph	You have hurt God, and *(emphatically)* you are going to be sorry.
Mary	I have not. Joseph, I am pure, I swear to it.
Joseph	If muddy water is crystal clear, I believe that you are pure. If the fragrance of a decomposed corpse is that of a flower, if worms and maggots make a tasty dish, I believe you are pure. So then, are you pure? *(sarcastically)* I believe you are pure.
Mary	The Lord is my judge.
Joseph	So he is indeed. He is mine too. He shall judge that man who gave you that child.
Mary	I have not known a man. I have not known… *(breaks down)* Why did the Lord choose me?
Joseph	Are those tears such as Delilah shed at Samson's feet? Then, I know them, Mary. Save them, for you may need some real ones in due course. For all intents and purposes, I consider you dead. You're done, we've reached the end of the road.
Mary	We've reached the end of the road. I am done; you consider me dead. *(Still crying)* All right, Joseph. If Zacharias could speak, he would warn you not to disbelieve. You may not have a tongue to lash your curse on me. (*Mary's mother enters. Her name is Charlotte. Mary continues now addressing her mom.*) Mom, you see what I have been reduced to. I have been called everything save a harlot. Your daughter who has been lifted by God has been lowered by man.

Charlotte   Your state, dearest daughter, is truly unsure. I believe and yet I don't. You have been looked upon in this town as a model. The epitome of morality. You preached it, Mary; you deplored the very appearance of immorality. But now look at what has happened, the tides are turned and the curse which you once directed to this town has sprung right back at you.

Mary   Mom, for you to treat me like this is unfair. To think this way of me is cruel.

Charlotte   Yet you did think of others in this same way. Just try to imagine what the whole township is thinking now. What you say now will not clear their thoughts. They'll just see you as the preacher who forgot to practice what she preached.

Mary   And when my Lord will find me guiltless, they'll all come stooping at my feet. The tides will turn again. It will not be just this town. The whole world will stoop beside me. How I magnify you, Oh mighty God. *(Sings or recites "The Magnificat" after which she says first verse of "I Am Alone")*

The Magnificat

My soul doth magnify the Lord,
And my spirit hath rejoiced in God my Savior
Because He hath regarded the humility of his handmaid:
for behold from henceforth all generations shall call me blessed.
Because He that is mighty hath done great
things to me, and holy is His name.
And His mercy is from generation unto
generations to them that fear Him.
He hath shewed might in His arm: He hath scattered
the proud in the conceit of their heart.
He hath put down the mighty from their
seat and hath exalted the humble.

He hath filled the hungry with good things,
and the rich He hath sent empty away.
He hath received Israel His servant, being mindful of His mercy.
As He spoke to our fathers; to Abraham and his seed forever.
Glory be to the Father, and to the Son, and to the Holy Ghost,
As it was in the beginning is now, and ever
shall be, world without end. Amen.
(Mary continues speaking)
I am alone, there's none who walks beside me
My one true Lord has thrown in the sea
I'm lost, I'm down, I'm everything that's wrong
A curse for life they think I ought to be
For why the reason I just cannot know
I just put my trust in Him who loves me so.

Joseph	Lord, have mercy. *(Mary's father enters; his name is Ephraim)*
Ephraim	Charlotte, Mary, holy greetings. How is it with you, son-in-law?
Joseph	Not to be anymore, sir. I couldn't have it.
Ephraim	Have it? Have what?
Joseph	Your daughter, sir. I could not have her hand anymore.
Ephraim	But, Joseph, you are engaged to her. You could not throw her down now. I would not have that.
Charlotte	Ephraim, we will have to be understanding. Joseph obviously thinks that our daughter is having another affair, and that's why she's with child.
Mary	But I've told you it is not so.
Ephraim	This is very deep and so we must think rationally. We need to look at all the possibilities in order to see if we can arrive at a compromise. Now, Joseph, the first thing you need to do is remove the block from your mind.

Charlotte	I wish this wasn't happening. Really can't we just know the truth?
Ephraim	Joseph, I specially asked Jepheth and Rhoda to come by this afternoon so we could try and work things out together in a peaceful manner which would leave everyone happy.
Joseph	My parents are coming here? But why?
Mary	To add to my pressure, I am sure.
Joseph	It will not help; my mind is already made up.
Charlotte	And what have you decided? Can it not change?
Joseph	No, I'm sorry, but I shall have to break off our engagement. This will be a nice, quiet, peaceful break which is how good old Ephraim would want it.
Ephraim	If that is to be, then let it be, but not before we have gone into this thoroughly.
Mary	I am sorry, but I do not want to be a part of this. May I take my leave. *(Holds her side)* Oh, my baby. *(exits)*
Ephraim	Mary, Mary, is she really gone?
Joseph	If she does not get the message now, she shall surely get it later anyhow. Let me go and tell her this. *(attempts to walk off)*
Charlotte	No, Joseph, stay right here. Just allow her to be by herself if this is what she wants.
Joseph	That's exactly what I am going to do; to tell her that as of now, she will be by herself, I'll be back.
Charlotte	Ephraim!
Ephraim	Charlotte!
Charlotte	What are we going to do?
Ephraim	We are left alone once more. To think that all was going so well, and everything was set for marriage. I can hardly see why this mess has come about.

Charlotte	Dear, we must admit that our daughter has brought disgrace on us and on our entire house. We must understand what Joseph is going through. They were both highly regarded, and it won't be long before this news breaks out. We may have to hide our faces, Ephraim. *(pause)* We shall have to sit Mary down and get the truth out of her. Honestly, this is not something we can take lightly. The bull, rather the cow, must be taken by the horns.
Ephraim	You do speak as one without heart or understanding. I cannot see that our daughter would insist on telling lies, and we must give her an ear. Charlotte, we are dealing with a God of Power, one who is almighty, all powerful. We are dealing with a God of miracles. Listen, do you recall that Abraham's wife Sarah conceived when she was past age? Was Hannah not thought to be barren until she conceived and gave birth to Samuel? Yet nearer home, have we not heard that Elizabeth is with child? Do you know what Elizabeth's age is? She is not a teenager, Charlotte. Elizabeth is gray, but God made it happen. We serve a God of miracles. Can you see? Do you not believe?
Charlotte	Yes, Ephraim, but…
Ephraim	Yes, Charlotte, let's suppose it is that the words of the prophet Esaias are realized this day. King Ahaz had asked for a sign…a sign…of some sort and the words of the prophet tell us now exactly what is happening… A virgin shall conceive and bear a son and shall call him Emmanuel. You do know that Scripture, do you not?
Charlotte	I do know it *(Joseph's parents enter. Their names are Jepheth and Rhoda)* those scriptures…hey, Godly ones. You must be terribly shaken.
Rhoda	I don't believe it; I am not believing it *(hysterically).*

Charlotte	Well, what exactly do you not believe? Mary? Joseph? Who?
Rhoda	That Mary, my sweet Mary could become involved in something like that; a charm of a girl she has been. I don't know how this could ever be.
Ephraim	Shall I start all over again in order to establish my daughter's chastity? The scriptures will bear me out.
Jepheth	It's just sad, so sad.
Charlotte	But look how close we got to seeing a beautiful marriage realized. Now it is not to be.
Jepheth	It's too bad, really bad.
Rhoda	Charlotte, we are not going to part company. Are we? There may be schism among the young, but not among the old.
Ephraim	My dear Rhoda, there can hardly be any schism of one kind or another. What God has ordained, he has ordained, and no powers on earth shall alter that. I believe that we are still to be the parents of two happily married young people.
Charlotte	Not with what is happening now, dear. Things have gotten out of hand. That is why Joseph has decided to break off the engagement.
Jepheth	He has? Oh dear, dear, dear.
Charlotte	He is determined that there is nothing that can prevent him from putting Mary away.
Rhoda	How can he do that?
Charlotte	Secretly, I imagine. He knows that he cannot afford to stir up any anxiety or excitement in the town. I don't know what Mary plans to do, but she may just need to have her baby and then go seek to find another husband.

Ephraim	Nonsense, I thought you had believed the scriptures. I am convinced that the passage in Esaias about the Virgin conceiving is in reference to Mary.
Jepheth	Well then, so let it be. Allow me, my brother and my sisters, to have my input on this most confusing and unbelievable issue. For me to say unbelievable could cause you to think that I am doubting God's power to work miraculously in our lives. Well, I'm not. My role here is to try to get us to think soberly and straight. It is evident that we are all still God-fearing people, and this makes my job so much easier. We are going to begin at the beginning, that is with Mary. You know Mary was a little girl who grew up so nicely, always attending the temple and becoming quite devout and Godfearing. While she grew, there were several…
Rhoda	Jepheth, we cannot take her biography now… at least not all of it.
Jepheth	Oh, hear me, hear me. Allow me to speak. I have remained quiet all this while and you have been talking. I think that I deserve a hearing.
Ephraim	Go on, my brother, speak.
Charlotte	But really, please don't go that far back.
Jepheth	Well, I'll just note that she would never have been thought of as one who would engage in any acts of immorality. I love my son, Joseph, but I love Mary too. I think I hear the voice of the prophet too. That sign…that sign.
Ephraim	I have been trying to say this for quite some time now. If therefore there is any doubt, we should give the benefit of the doubt to Mary.

Charlotte

If you insist on taking this stand, then what can I say? I may as well fall in. If it is Mary to whom the prophet refers, then surely there is cause for rejoicing. But I cannot see… Why would God choose one who is of such a lowly status, one such as Mary to be Mother of the Savior of the Word? Would He choose to come to such a community, such an unknown town. We are not even on the map!

Jepheth

But we are going to get there now. Mary's going to bring us some fame.

Ephraim

Oh, I wish she would.

Rhoda

I don't know. I just do not know. My poor Mary.

Jepheth

Oh, let us be Merry.

Ephraim

Set sorrow aside.

Rhoda
and Charlotte

Will Jesus our Savior be born on this tide? *(they all sing adapted version of hymn, first verse only)*

A virgin most pure as the prophets do tell
Shall bring forth a baby as it hath befell
To be our redeemer from death, hell and sin
Which Adam's transgression hat wrapped us in.
And therefore, be merry, set sorrow aside
Christ Jesus our Savior to be born on this tide

(Lights go dim. Choral group comes on stage.
They continue telling story.)
Now all the pain and sorrow too
Had disappeared as nights went through
The sadness really turned to joy
And now the little boy
Of whom the prophet spoke the very best
Would be different from all the rest

How could they tell what was to be?
It seemed that only God could see.
They struggled on with this whole thing

In spite of what you heard them sing
A long debate of course ensued
Until they thought they must conclude

This young lady plagued by tears
And who had not lived many years
Was sweet and innocent and pure
Of this they all became quite sure
Meanwhile days and nights had gone ahead
And thoughts were changed as we have said

To Joseph, an angel did appear
And quickly vanished his dreaded fear
They spoke in signs and visions most
That Mary conceived of the Holy Ghost
Don't put her away Joseph was told
Still keep her tight within your fold

And so, we pick up the act again
Please note the scene remains the same
But time has gone on by weeks and days
So whatever happened be not amazed
The Lord did speak out from the skies
and opened up their half-closed eyes
So now they start to make their plan
Just how to greet the Son of Man

(Joseph enters in a most exciting mood. He virtually ignores the others.)

Joseph	I don't believe it. I cannot… Of course, I believe it *(turning to the others)* Believe me, I believe!
Charlotte	Tell us your story, my son. Did the Lord really appear to you?
Joseph	Oh, most certainly He did. I am so excited to tell you what happened. All I know is that I am most special in the eyes of God. He has selected me to be the earthly father of the Savior of the world. Now tell me, goodly folk, do I deserve this?

Rhoda	You are worthy, my boy. That is why the Lord selected you. Mary is quite worthy too.
Joseph	But look at how I behaved, so badly. I am so ashamed of myself. I judged Mary. I cursed, I swore, I doubted. Can God still use one like me for His purpose? I hurt Mary so much. Will she ever forgive me?
Ephraim	You really hurt my daughter. Yes, you did. And we were all upset, but how can we be angry with you when you were carrying the burdens of uncertainties and the pains of jealously.
Rhoda	I just want to thank the Lord; I just want to thank the Lord.
Jepheth	My dear son. You make us so proud of you. I have been almost without speech before I got the assurance that God really did appear to you. Your grandfather before me always said that if God who rescued our forefathers from the Egyptians is still alive, then any bad deed can be made good. You have shown us that this God is still alive.
Charlotte	Does Mary know about all this? How does she feel about what has happened? Tell us truly. What did the Angel say? Where were you? What were you doing? What else happened?
Joseph	As you well know, I was troubled for weeks. I was totally confused and my ego was completely destroyed. For a while, I thought that I was not a man. I felt that I had made a serious mistake choosing Mary as my life's partner. I was so harsh on her, and I started to make the final plans as to how I was going to end the engagement. I called Mary, and we spoke about it several times at length but she just could not accept that it was God's will for us to go our separate ways. I got angry every time, but she insisted that she was pure.

Until finally, I went to bed one night, bent on running away the next morning to a place as far as I could get. That was the very night when the Lord spoke. *(He sings)*

<u>An Angel Came to Me</u>

While I was sleeping in my bed
An angel came to me and said
Joseph, Joseph, hear me please
This news will set your mind at ease
Mary will have a baby boy
And he will fill the earth with joy
The Holy Ghost has done this deed
But he'll be yours for you to feed

Cho.
Call him, call him, call him Jesus
Call him, call him, call him Lord
I got awake and looked around
But no one in sight could be found
I'm from the Lord and I must tell
I am the Angel Gabriel
Mary will have a baby boy
And he will fill the earth with joy
Don't put her down and cause a strife
Still take her home to be your wife.

Cho.
Call him, call him, call him Jesus
Call him, call him, call him Lord
Charlotte: So then, where is Mary now? Dreaming too?

Joseph	No, she left to go visit with her cousin Elizabeth. Of course, you know that God worked miraculously in their lives too. Elizabeth became pregnant at such an old age, and she has already given birth to a son. Mary should be back any time now. But we have made it all up. We have reconciled. I just hope that the Lord will forgive me for hurting her baby so badly.
Ephraim	Is Zacharias all right? Did I hear correctly that he had lost his speech?
Joseph	Yes, he did lose his speech because of unbelief, but now he has it all back again.
Rhoda	But we can hardly take the time to hear about these elderly folks now. I want to hear about Mary and how she is doing.
Jepheth	Patience, patience. These are righteous and devout people too. Should we not have some interest in them?
Ephraim	I suppose so. Charlotte, it might soon be our turn to experience God's miraculous acts. *(They all chuckle).*
Charlotte	But how could Zacharias receive his speech back just like that. Some strange things are happening in this town, and I do not know just when and where it will end.
Joseph	It does seem as if it was thus ordained; Zacharias just lost his speech, and it was only to return to him after the birth of John.
Rhoda	John? Who is that?
Joseph	Oh, John is the name Zacharias was instructed to call the child. He, in fact, wrote this on a scroll before he regained his speech. So the boy has a name, and all three are just fine.
Jepheth	Ephraim, let us take a trip to see these Godly folks and their miracle baby. What do you think?

Ephraim	That surely is a most kind and splendid thought. We could sit in my carriage. I just gave it a nice good cleaning.
Jepheth	Very well, let me go look at the first of the miracle babies. *(They exit)*
Joseph	And mine will be the second miracle baby.
Rhoda	No, Charlotte. They shall not leave us. I don't know about you, but they are not leaving me… Hey, fellows, wait, we are coming. Hold on. Come, Charlotte. *(They too exit) (Joseph sings by himself).*
Joseph	*(singing "Yes, God Is Good in Earth and Sky" or another appropriate piece)*

Yes, God is good: in earth and sky,
From ocean's depths and spreading wood,
Ten thousand voices seem to cry,
God made us all, and God is good.

The sun that keeps his trackless way,
And downward pours his golden flood,
Night's sparkling hosts, all seem to say,
In accents clear, that God is good.

The merry birds prolong the strain,
Their song with ev'ry spring renewed;
And balmy air, and falling rain,
Each softly whispers, God is good.

Yes, God is good, all nature says,
By God's own hand with speech endued;
And man, in louder notes of praise,
Should sing for joy that God is good.

For all Thy gifts we bless Thee, Lord,
But chiefly for our heavenly food;
Thy pardoning grace, Thy quickening word,
These prompt our song that God is good.

(Mary enters from the other side).

Mary

My darling.

Joseph

My sweet Mary *(He comes toward her and embraces her.)*, I have treated you so badly. I have been awful. I have just about ruined your reputation and your good image.

Mary

Well, what? What should I tell you?

Joseph

(taking her by the hand and leading her to a seat) Let me take you and sit you down, my dear. I hardly know where to begin making my apologies and seeking your forgiveness. *(He sits her down.)* Now, Mary, you know that life is full of surprises and uncertainties. At the same time, one may never know when it is his turn. No one can tell how much things can change in a matter of…

Act II, Scene I

The Inn. Sim and Todd are workers in the Inn. Lois is their supervisor but interacts with them at their level. They are not too busy when the scene opens, so they are just snacking and talking casually. They have congregated at the front and eating snacks. Japhat is the owner of the Inn. Ben and Rachel are a couple who also wanted to stay at the inn.

Tod	*(Biting into some food)* Oh my word; oh wow! This is good stuff. Lois, I love every taste of it. I wish you would take food for us more often. You are so great at cooking.
Sim	That is truly Mr. Greedy *(Looking at Tod)*. You eat so much here…like you do not get to eat at home.
Tod	Only when it is food cooked by Lois. It is irresistible. Could I have some more, please?
Lois	Tod, you are my biggest culinary fan. You compliment me even on my worst dishes *(Laughs)* Ha! Ha! Ha!
Sim	I remember one time when…*(There is a knock on the door)*… Someone's outside… Let me go and deal with it. *(He goes to the door and strikes up a conversation with a couple who wants to stay there for the night.)* Hello, sir, and greetings to you, madam. I will be happy to assist you today.
Ben	Oh, thank you. We were hoping to make it to our place of abode tonight, but we were delayed on the way, and now we are feeling so tired.
Sim	I am sorry about that…that is too bad.

Rachel	This really seems like a comfortable place for us to stay, so we are looking forward to the opportunity… We would like to stay here for the night.
Sim	Oh dear me. I think that we may have a problem here.
Rachel	Problem? What problem? Please, sir!
Ben	I am sure that you can solve the problem.
Sim	I wish that I could. We have been overbooked… really fully booked for the last two weeks. There is not even one room available.
Ben	Oh no! I hope that you are joking.
Sim	I wish I was, but…really… I am not the person in charge here. Lois is in charge.
Rachel	Who?
Sim	My supervisor is Lois; she makes all the decisions here.
Ben	Do you mean that she owns the inn? I am happy she is female. This means that she would have a soft heart.
Sim	No! No! NO! I mean no…she does not own the inn. Japhat does, but he has…kind of…turned everything over to her. *(whispers)* By the way, her heart is not too soft. She has turned away three wornout travelers. You may even be the fourth. *(Ben and Rachel look at each other)*
Ben	*(reluctantly)* Do you think that I could try to persuade her?
Sim	No, that is not going to work…but let me go and see what I can do. *(He steps away and goes over to the section of the stage where Tod and Lois are sitting in darkness. The Light now comes on to highlight them.)*
Sim	*(Addressing Lois)* Well. What do you think?
Lois	Think? Think about what?

Sim	Another travelling worn-out couple. Ever since the government closed down the other two inns in this town, there has been a lot of pressure on us to find room for people who are visiting.
Lois	So what? That is not my problem!
Tod	Gosh! You do get into a foul mood whenever you are stressed out, Lois.
Lois	*(Looking at Sim)* So what is the issue? Let us just get it out of the way.
Sim	I was just wondering if there is any way that we could squeeze and make some space for that couple. They seem to be such lovely folk.
Lois	*(Standing and glaring at Sim)* Look at me and look at me good. *(emphatically)* Read...my... lips! The inn is full. Okay? Please go and send them on their way.
Tod	*(To Sim)* I told you she is a hard taskmaster!
Sim	*(Walking slowly toward couple, then turns around and looks at Lois and speaks once more to her)* Okay, ma'am...if you say so. *(He then approaches couple, but they already sensed what has happened.)*
Rachel	*(To Sim)* Is the news good? I am trying to read your face.
Sim	I am sorry, but you will need to keep traveling. It will be a long time before you may even find a good place to rest... But good luck! *(Ben holds Rachel's hand and turns away, walking slowly.)* *(Group comes on for choral/verse speaking)*

So ON and On and ON and ON
Until all the workers' strength was gone
the travelers were turned away
No one else was allowed to stay
"We're full," "we're packed," "we're booked right out"

The stressed-out workers would all shout
So please don't even try to test
for in this Inn, there'll be no rest
One worker was mean; another tired
So many guests just cried and cried
but if you think these guests were cursed
for one special couple, things just got worse
(Verse speakers leave stage. Lois, Sim, and Tod continue their conversation.)

Tod	So we look like the mean ones while the owner of this inn hides in the back and pushes us out front.
Sim	This is what I was thinking too. It is so unfair.
Lois	That old Japhat. You both know how I cannot stand the guy. I tell you that it will just be a matter of time, and I will be out of here.
Tod	You mean that you are going to quit?
Lois	Of course! Who wants to stay and work under this oppressive and stressful situation while the big coward hides away? We are the ones who get the stares and the glares and the abuse from the public.
Sim	Well, if you quit, I am going to quit too. Tod will have a great time running this inn all by himself. Ha! Ha! Ha!
Tod	*(sarcastically)* You're right. Do not even think about it. Anyway, why don't we put up that sign at the front door?
Sim	What sign?
Tod	The one that says "All Rooms Occupied." That will deter persons from even stopping. That would certainly be easier than having us trying to explain to every passerby who stops by to enquire.

Sim	Great idea! Lois, what do you think?
Lois	I do not even care what you do. Do whatever you want and keep it there forever.
Sim	Lois!
Lois	What? I do not care whether this inn is full or empty. So let us end the stress now. Tod, go ahead and put that sign up. You can even lock the doors if you feel like it.
Tod	I will do just that, then I will start to eat again. *(He goes off to pick up the sign and places it in an appropriate place.)*
Sim	Yes. That will do it. Now we shall have some peace and quiet around here.
Lois	What a relief? Japhat will get the message. He has been promising to build additional rooms at this inn, but as usual, he is just Talk! Talk! Talk!
Tod	*(Returning to center stage)* It is done! Yeah! Yippee! Yippityyap. Hey, Lois, is it about time for us to start eating again? *(He reaches for a snack. In the meantime, Joseph and a heavily pregnant Mary approaches the inn and looks relieved.)*
Joseph	This must be it now, Mary. We are here at last.
Mary	Oh, thank goodness. I could not go another mile, not even an inch.
Joseph	You will be fine, my dear Mary. Our God has given you just enough strength to make it this far. *(He looks up and sees the sign)* Look, Mary! Look!
Mary	Oh, Joseph, please do not scare me; if you get me too excited—*(She looks up and sees the sign)* Oh no! Are you kidding me? This must be a big joke!
Joseph	I am not even going to wait until someone comes over to the desk. You are heavy with child. You need attention now.

Mary	But the sign says "All Rooms Occupied!" Oh, Joseph. What are we going to do?
Joseph	God is going to protect us. They will have a soft spot in their heart for you, especially with one in your situation. *(He knocks on the door)*
Mary	Joseph. You are such a great husband. I wish they would come now. *(Joseph goes over to hug her, and she leans over on him. Lois comes toward them.)* Oh, here they come. It is a woman. She will be nice. Thanks be to God! *(Lois approaches with a straight angry face)*
Lois	How can I help you? We are all tired and stressed out here.
Joseph	Well, I am really so sorry about that. Anyway, we are looking for a room to stay tonight. It has been a long journey for us.
Lois	Can you read, sir?
Joseph	What do you mean? Of course, I can!
Lois	Good. And do you speak English?
Joseph	Well, I guess… I am just asking for a room
Lois	*(Impatiently)* And that sign says it all. Just read it; there is no room. The sign says "All Rooms Occupied." Now say it with me. All… Rooms…
Joseph	I am not believing this… I am not believing this *(emphatically)* My wife is pregnant!
Lois	*(sarcastically)* That is too bad. Oh dear! Oh dear!
Mary	*(Crying)* I am going to have a baby
Lois	This has nothing to do with babies. We just cannot accommodate anyone else in this inn tonight. We are full tonight. Really sorry
Joseph	Well, can you try to squeeze…?
Lois	Sounds like you neither read nor understand English.
Joseph	*(angrily)* Is there anyone with a heart around here? Does anyone care? We need help! We are worn out! We are tired! We are God's people!

Mary	*(beginning to cry)* Do not yell, Joseph. Our God will not be pleased.
Joseph	*(Crying too)* Oh my gosh! I lost my cool; I am so sorry, Mary, but this is so cruel. *(Japhat, the owner of the inn, walks in)*
Japhat	Why all this noise and chaos? Lois! Can you tell me why we are having all this commotion?
Lois	Truth be known, you created the problem… You are the problem…
Japhat	Now wait a minute! What are you saying?
Lois	You were the one who refused to add new rooms, you were the one who asked us to close the doors on persons who are seeking accommodation regardless of the circumstances, and now you want to know what is the issue? *(She sarcastically repeats the question which he asked her back to him verbatim)* Why all this noise and chaos? Lois. Can you tell me why we are having all this commotion?
Joseph	Sir, if you are the owner here, can you find it in your heart to help my wife find a place to have her baby?
Lois	*(addressing Japhat)* Yes. You created the problem! You deal with it! I am out of here.
Mary	Oh, this pain is becoming unbearable. I need to sit down and relax. Sir, are you going to help us?
Japhat	If they tell you that the inn is full, then it is really full; I really do not know what else to do for you.
Joseph	*(Holding Mary)* Mary, let us be on our way. We may have our baby on the side of the road. But we know that our God will protect us.

(He sings song, "God of Our Fathers")

God of Our Fathers whose almighty hand
You'll come in pow'r and you'll reach every land
You made the world and gave us all we need
We will not faint but follow as you lead

You've called us both to help you with your plan
To bring Salvation now to every man
Help us to know that You will lead us on
as now we seek a place to birth your son

So onward we go, just let us know your will
We're in your hands; our calling to fulfill
Increase our faith; our trust is all in you
We give you thanks; we know your word is true

Protect and guide your servants now we pray
Grant us your peace as we live day by day
Right now, it seems that we don't know your way
but we know for sure, we'll find a place to stay.

Japhat	If you are really that desperate, there is a place where I could have you both stay *(Mary's and Joseph's face light up)*
Joseph	Oh of course! Please! We will sleep anywhere
Japhat	Do not be so sure about that…that you will sleep anywhere… I am talking about a…umm…it is kind of…
Mary	Kind of…does not matter. Please show us where it is.
Japhat	It is in the stable. About…
Joseph	You are too humorous, you are so funny… But we do need comic relief now.
Japhat	Really! I am not joking. Our stables are fairly clean. I could have you stay in one of the newly built sections if that works for you. There may even be one which has not had any animals live there as of yet.
Joseph	So we are going to be staying with oxen and donkey and sheep?
Japhat	I told you that you were not going to like it. You really do not have to stay there, but honestly, that is all we have.

Mary   Joseph, let us go and see what he is talking about. God
                 chose us to be the parents of the savior of the world.
                 He will not leave us without His help

                 (Choir sings "Away in a Manger")

                 Away in a manger
                 No crib for a bed
                 The little Lord Jesus
                 Laid down His sweet head
                 The stars in the bright sky
                 Looked down where He lay
                 The little Lord Jesus
                 Asleep on the hay

                 The cattle are lowing
                 The Baby awakes
                 But little Lord Jesus
                 No crying He makes
                 I love You, Lord Jesus
                 Look down from the sky
                 And stay by my side
                 Until morning is nigh

Joseph   I suppose so…we will go

Japheth   Okay, let's go this way… *(They move toward the door
                 to the stable; Choir sings from "Thou Didst Leave
                 Thy Throne and Thy Kingly Crown." This may also
                 be a prerecorded presentation.)*

                 Thou didst leave Thy throne and thy kingly crown,
                 When Thou camest to earth for me;
                 But in Bethlehem's home was there found no room
                 For Thy holy nativity:

                 Cho
                 Oh, come to my heart, Lord Jesus!
                 There is room in my heart for Thee;

Heaven's arches rang when the angels sang,
Proclaiming Thy royal degree;
But of lowly birth cam'st Thou, Lord, on earth,
And in great humility:

The foxes found rest, and the birds had their nest
In the shade of the forest tree;
But Thy couch was the sod, O Thou Son of God,
In the deserts of Galilee:

Thou camest, O Lord, with the living Word
That should set Thy people free;
But with mocking scorn, and with crown of thorn,
They bore Thee to Calvary:

Oh, come to my heart, Lord Jesus!
Thy cross is my only plea;

When heavens arches shall ring, and her choirs shall sing
At Thy coming to victory,
Let Thy voice calls me up, saying, "Yet there is room,
There is room at My side for thee!"
And my heart shall rejoice Lord Jesus,
When Thou comest and callest for me.
(End of scene)

Act II, Scene II
The Shepherd's Cabin

(Four shepherds are huddled together around a fireplace. They are having a causal conversation and discussing the day's activities. Their names are Nashon, Hezron, Jotham, Zadok.)

Nashon	This has been a rough day. I am so glad that it is finally over.
Hezron	Oh, brother. It was for me too. I just barely made it back here to the cabin.
Nashon	There was not even much of an opportunity to relax and unwind; those wild beasts are on the loose.
Jotham	Did you see me chasing one away while still hiding behind a rock? I had given up on my life, but I escaped.
Hezron	I have had that experience. It can be so scary, man. Real dangerous to protect these sheep. But I guess we have to do what we need to do.
Zadok	Hey, fellows, when you talk about scary, let me tell you about it. A few from my flock were under attack today. I must have fallen asleep or dozed off for a little while. It is so embarrassing that I am not sure if I even want to talk about it.
Nashon	You mean that the beasts got inside?
Zadok	No. It was not that bad. I was moving from one pasture to another and I seemed to have missed one sheep.
Jotham	What do you mean, bro? You're missing one sheep? We will help you find it.

Hezron	I do not want to make light of this, but we all have sheep go astray from time to time. I would not worry too much about it.
Jotham	With Zadok, it is different though. He gets really attached. They are like his children. *(Addressing Zadok)* Was it just one sheep that went astray?
Nashon	I am thinking that we should go and help recover this sheep. We have always been a team here.
Zadok	Oh, that would be so nice. I have a little sense of the direction that we would need to look.
Nashon	Okay, why don't Zadok and I go in search of that sheep while Hezron and Jotham will stay here and keep an eye on those which are already secure?
Hezron	I can live with that.
Jotham	Sounds like a plan to me
Nashon	Okay, brothers, we are on the move.
Jotham	See you later, fellows. *(They get up, and after a few steps, a bright light flashes.)*
Zadok	Oh, wait a minute! What was that?
Hezron	*(shouting)* Did you all see that?
Nashon	Something is happening here! Something very strange. *(Bright light comes on again and flashes at longer spells)*
Jotham	Oh no! No! No! Somebody save us! What about the sheep? Who is going to save the sheep? *(They all get up to run. As they start running, the bright light comes on and stays on. All four of them fall to the ground in fear and trembling. They all make unintelligible sounds for upward of thirty seconds. The sounds get softer as the voice of the angel is heard.)*

Angel's Voice	Hey, all ye good men! Stay in your places. I have some good news to tell.
Nashon	What is this? What is happening?
Zadok	We are all okay. Please go away.
Angel's Voice	I cannot go away. I am from the Lord God!
Zadok	So who are you? Where are you? We cannot see you!
Hezron	*(Whispering to other shepherds)* Be quiet, all of you! Are you not afraid? Our lives are going to end. We have fallen into the claws of some wild beast.
Jotham	This sounds like more than a wild beast to me. I am deeply afraid. I am really fearful *(increased decibel)*. I am terrified!
Angel's Voice	Oh, do not be afraid! For behold I bring you good news that will cause great joy for all the people. Good news! Good news! Good news! *(Up to a crescendo)* Good tidings of great joy.
Nashon	What is your name? What is this good news? We are all having a panic attack here.
Angel's Voice	Relax and be merry, everyone. No one is going to hurt you. You are all in good hands!
Jotham	So go ahead and tell us what you have to tell us. Please do not keep us in suspense any longer. This is… *(Softens his voice)*Oh so scary!
Angel's Voice	I will say it one more time. Do not be afraid! None of you! The good news… The good news is that today… On this day in the town of David, a Savior has been born to you. A savior who is Christ, the Lord. He is the Messiah. He is Lord.
Hezron	A Savior who is Christ the Lord? *(Ponders)* A Savior who is Christ the Lord!
Nashon	A Savior who is Christ the Lord?
Zodak	For unto us is born this day?
Jotham	A Savior who is Christ the Lord?

Angel's Voice	Yes. A Savior who is Christ the Lord. He has been born on this glorious day. And this will be a sign to you. You will find the baby wrapped in swaddling clothes and lying in a manger.
Zodak	This is waking me up!
Angel's Voice	All of Israel needs to wake up. The people who walked in darkness have seen a great light. On those living in the land of the shadow of death; upon them the light has dawned. Anyway, I need to go. You have all heard the good news.
Jotham	No! Don't go! Please stay here with us.
Angel's Voice	I must be gone! Duty calls! Many more must hear the good news too. Please you must go and spread this glorious news too. I am a herald! You must be heralds too *(echo of "Be Heralds Too" until it fades; choir or other singing group sings "Hark the Herald Angels Sing" and "Angels We Have Heard on High")* Shepherds continue their conversation. Say in unison: Gloria, Gloria, Gloria, Gloria…glory to God in the highest, Gloria, Gloria, Gloria, Gloria… Glory to God in the highest, glory be to God on high, and on earth, peace and goodwill to all people, we praise thee; we worship thee, we bless thee, we glorify thee, we give thanks to thee for thy great glory. Oh Lord God, Heavenly King, God the Father Almighty; for thou only art holy, thou only art the Lord. Oh lord the only begotten son, Jesus Christ oh lord God, Lamb of God, Son of the Father, thou only art the Lord; thou that takest away the sin of the world, have mercy upon us.

| | Thou that takest away the sin of he world, receive our prayer; thou that sittest at the right hand of God, the Father, have mercy upon us. For thou only art holy. Thou only, o Christ, with the holy ghost, art Most High in the glory of God the Father. |

Hezron

Do we believe what we just heard? Was this real or was this a dream?

Zadok

It sounded real to me, but it is still hard to believe. But... What did we read about in the book of Esias *(Isaiah)* For behold a virgin shall conceive and give birth to a son and his name shall be called Emanuel? Can we not believe? Do we not believe?

NASHON

Well, as for me, believe me, I believe. We just heard it from the writings of Esias. The people who walked in darkness hath seen a great light... the virgin shall conceive and give birth to a son. It has happened. The long-awaited Messiah has finally come *(sings solo of "Come Thou Long Expected Jesus")*

Come, Thou long expected Jesus
Born to set Thy people free;
From our fears and sins release us,
Let us find our rest in Thee.

Israel's strength and consolation,
Hope of all the earth Thou art;
Dear desire of every nation,
Joy of every longing heart.

Born Thy people to deliver,
Born a child and yet a King,
Born to reign in us forever,
Now Thy gracious kingdom bring.

By Thine own eternal Spirit
Rule in all our hearts alone;
By Thine all sufficient merit,
Raise us to Thy glorious throne.

Hezron	Oh, believe me, I believe. What a phenomenon?
Jotham	I kind of believe, yet I would want to go and see for myself.
Hezron	You want to see what?
Jotham	The Baby. That's what the herald said. This will be a sign to you…you shall find the babe wrapped in swaddling clothes and lying in a manger.
Hezron	That was not just an ordinary herald. That was the angel of God.
Jotham	What difference does it make? That is what the man said. That is what we heard.
Nashon	But can we go? Do we know the way?
Zadok	No! We can't go! Who is going to watch over the sheep?
Hezron	The sheep will be fine. They will be protected by the God of Our Fathers. He is the God of Abraham, Isaac, and Jacob. We will also be protected by that same God. Who wants to go? Anyone coming?
Nashon	I still, ask! How can we know the way?
Jotham	By His light, Our God will lead us to the right place. At other times, He has used a star to guide His people. We know that He will do the same for us now.
Nashon	A star? A star? Oh yes, a star. I think that we have really seen enough signs to believe that the predictions of scripture have come to pass. I think that we should all go.

Zadok

Let us now go even unto Bethlehem and see this thing which has come to pass. Which the angel has made known unto us…
(Choir or other singing group sing the carol "While Shepherds Watched Their Flocks by Night." Toward the end of the song, sung or prerecorded, shepherds leave stage to embark on their journey.)
(End of scene)

Act II, Scene III

Outside in the courtyard of Herod's Palace near the balcony. King Herod, his wife Priscilla, and Josiah, an attendant, are discussing what they deemed to be strange and mysterious events. They are standing on stage with faded lights as prerecorded version of "We Three Kings" is played/sung. Light brightens on stage toward end of song. Herod is pacing the floor anxiously.

Herod	*(nervously, anxiously, and astonishingly)* They followed a star? A star led them to the place where he was born? He was born in a manger?
Josiah	Truly, Oh King, that is exactly what happened.
Herod	And then, what happened? Did they really find a baby? But how can He be a king?
Josiah	They found Him O King…they found him… and when they did, He was lying in swaddling clothes. When they found Him, He was lying in a manger.
Priscilla	Mystery of Mysteries. Oh, how can this be?
Herod	My queen, are you okay?
Priscilla	I do not know, Oh King. You do not seem to be okay either.
Herod	I am deeply troubled. I am troubled to the core. I feel betrayed. I feel threatened. I feel like I am going to lose my mind.
Josiah	And for good reason, Oh King. I understand, Oh King! Oh King, I will always be loyal to you. I could never do what they did.
Priscilla	Tell me, Josiah; who are we talking about? And what did whoever it is do?

Josiah	My Queen, they followed the star until it stopped over where the young king lay.
Herod	*(anxiously)* King? Did you say young king?
Josiah	Yes, Oh King. I mean no, Oh King… I did not say king… I did not believe… I did not mean to say king. The star stopped over the place where the young child lay.
Herod	Oh! What a relief.
Priscilla	So what did they do after that?
Josiah	They bowed down and they worshiped the newborn king and they…
Herod	You said it again, Josiah *(in a higher decibel)*. You said it again. Will you stop calling him a king?
Josiah	Oh, King! They worshipped the little baby.
Priscilla	They did what?
Josiah	They worshipped the baby, oh Queen, and gave Him gifts… Well, they handed the gifts of gold and frankincense and myrrh to His parents. They thought that that was their way of honoring the king. Oops! I am sorry, Oh King. They think that the little baby boy is a king. But you are the only king… Oh King.
Priscilla	Set of traitors!
Josiah	Oh King, you are not going to lose your throne… but if you were to lose your throne… Herod *(raising his voice)* Oh stop, Josiah! Stop! Do you understand? *(Reuben and Leah enter. They are the prince and princess and heirs to the throne. They were overhearing the conversation all along.)*
Reuben	Oh, Papa King, Dear Mama Queen, Leah and I heard what you were talking about and Leah is not happy. She is sad.
Leah	*(addressing Reuben)* You are sad too, Reuben. It is not just me. I do not even want to cry *(starts crying)*

Reuben	Please tell her not to cry *(starts crying too)*. It seems as if we are going to lose our place in the palace. Papa King, Is this really going to happen?
Josiah	Oh King. This is so sad for our young prince and young princess. We need to do something to make them feel happy.
Leah	*(still sobbing)* Why can't we just take the young baby in here to live with us? I would love to take care of a little sister.
Reuben	It is a baby boy, Leah. He can come to live here, but I still want to be prince.
Herod	You will remain prince, my son. Leah, you will always be my princess.
Priscilla	That is positive thinking, but our prince and princess will never remain in this palace if the gods choose to place another king here!
Herod	My queen. *(Walks toward her and holds her)* My Dear Queen, that is not going to happen.
Josiah	Oh King, I do not want that to happen either… yet I wonder why it is that so many of our own are making the trip to go and visit this baby.
Reuben	That is why I am so sad. Leah and I want the baby to come and live at the palace with us. That way, we will all be happy. Right, Leah?
Leah	That would be so nice, Papa King. Please let him do it, Mama Queen!
Herod	It cannot work that way, my princess.
Priscilla	So what are we going to do?
Herod	I have a plan; I know what I am going to do.
Reuben	What is your plan, Papa King?
Herod	I have a plan…a plan that will take blood.
Priscilla	Blood?
Josiah	Blood, Oh King?
Reuben	Blood, Papa King?
Leah	Blood, Papa King?

Herod	Yes. You all heard me. I am going to take blood! I am going to issue a decree! I want all the youth in the land to be slain. No questions asked! Just kill them. All!
Priscilla	Are you out of your mind, dear King? How could you do that?
Leah	*(starts crying again)* Papa King. You are not going to kill us. We are your own flesh and blood.
Herod	No, my princess. I could never kill my own. You two are my precious little ones.
Reuben	*(Proudly and boastfully)* We are so special. We are royal blood. No one can touch royal blood.
Priscilla	Still, this plan is a non-starter. If we tried to kill all the youth in the land, there is bound to be another rebellion in the land. People might take to the streets and then we might really be overthrown.
Josiah	Oh, My Queen, when the King speaks, the whole world will tremble and take heed. Let us hear him out.
Herod	*(in a loud commanding voice)* And I say…and I say…every male youth in this land who is fifteen years and under will be slain. None will be spared.
Leah	Papa King. My brother! My brother!
Herod	With the exception of my own flesh and blood. Reuben only will be spared.
Reuben	*(running out and crying)* I do not want to be a part of this. I do not want to live here any longer.
Priscilla	Oh King, can we try and work this out without hurting our own?
Herod	I already said that Reuben will not be touched.
Priscilla	But he is already disturbed. You saw it with your own eyes and heard it with your own ears.

Leah	Oh, Mama Queen; I will go see after Reuben. *(She starts toward door and then turns around and addresses Herod.)* Oh, Papa King. You do not want to have blood on your hands. You really don't. *(Turns around and exits stage)*
Josiah	Oh, My King and oh My Queen. This is one bloody mess that we are in.
Herod	Josiah, we cannot just keep talking or nothing will happen. My throne is threatened, and I will have to take action.
Priscilla	Can we not wait to see if this is even true?
Herod	No. We cannot afford to wait or then it is going to be too late. We cannot close the gate after the horse has already gone through.
Josiah	Oh, Queen. It is all true. There are just so many signs…
Herod	*(in a stern voice)* Okay enough. I am issuing a decree now. All male youths, fifteen and under, must be killed on sight. Josiah, please go call the men.
Priscilla	Why do we even need to kill fifteen-year-olds? If it is an infant, it will take a long time before he gets to age fifteen.
Josiah	Oh King, if I may speak, I would suggest to you, Oh King, what I think would be a good plan. Since our queen has reminded us that the boy is just an infant, why don't we lower the age to ten years? That would be so much less work on the troops. It would also…
Herod	Oh Josiah. You are so wise. You have spoken well.
Priscilla	If we are going to shed blood, I still think that ten years of age is still too high a bar. There is only one child King so…
Herod	King? Did you say child king too?

Priscilla	Oh King. You know that your rule comes with a lot of weight; your rule comes with a lot of authority. I would say let the bar be five years. Let us make it so that all infants under the age of five years will be slain.
Herod	Let me consider this well. *(He finally sits down.)* When was this child born?
Josiah	I do not know, Oh King, but it is far less than five years. It really has been just only days ago. Maybe a few weeks at most.
Herod	A few weeks ago, at most? *(Ponders repeatedly).* A few weeks ago, at most. Well, then here is my plan. I am not going to slay anyone who is over five years old. As a matter of fact, I am only going to slay all infants who are two years old and under.
Priscilla	Not all infants, Oh King. This baby is a boy. You do not have to slay even one girl in this land.
Herod	But how can we be sure that it is a boy? Josiah, can you help us with this? We do not want to go on a killing spree and then miss the main target.
Josiah	Oh King, I can share with confidence that it was a baby boy that was born. Hence, we can spare all the girls.
Herod	Very well then. It is all settled. My mind is made up, so here is my decree. Starting tonight, all the male infants in this land who are two years old or under will be slain. It is done. Josiah, go give the orders out and make sure that all the troops hear.
Josiah	At your word, sir. By your word, Oh King. These orders shall be carried out
Herod	*(shouting)* And starting tonight.
Josiah	I have heard you, Oh King. It shall be so. *(Josiah leaves with quick sharp steps)*
Priscilla	I still do not know that this is the right thing to do. I am kind of troubled.

Herod	Troubled? Why would you be troubled, My Queen?
Priscilla	I am a mother, O King. And already I am feeling the pain of all mothers.
Herod	If we do not act this way, then we are going to feel the pain of being overthrown by a child king.
Priscilla	King? Did you say king?
Herod	Call him what you will. Very soon, he will be no more. I just want him numbered among the slain.
Priscilla	And what if we do not get the blood of this infant?
Herod	What?
Priscilla	How do we know for sure that we are going to find this infant who is a threat to your throne? It could be that we are fighting against the gods.
Herod	Well, I am doing the best that I can. I am sure that I can come up with another plan if this one does not work. *(Josiah enters excitedly.)*
Josiah	I greet you, O King. I greet you, O Queen. The king's word has been delivered. The decree has been issued. The horses are ready; the men have been all mounted. Swords in their shields; breastplates in place; the plan is set to roll; the blood shall flow; and the child will be dead.
Priscilla	This is too much, O King. I am so sorry that I was a part of this. I do not know if we did the right thing. O King, I must depart. I must go and lay myself down. I am not sure if I did the right thing. *(She turns and departs stage.)*
Herod	I am alone, there is none who walks beside me; my one true love has thrown me in the sea. I am lost, I am done; I am everything that's wrong… I am not sure if I have done the right thing. Sings solo "I Don't Know If I Did the Right Thing."

Herod's Song

I don't know if I did the right thing
So this is the song I will sing
My throne's under threat
Now I am starting to fret
And soon, I will no longer be king.

I don't know if I'll stand or I'll fall
So now I will just get them all
Whatever it takes
And now for my ego's Sake
For sure, I will still need to stand tall

I don't know if I'll live or I'll die
So I might tell this world goodbye
That little boy child
Though he is gentle and mild
Will die, and all the world will know why

(End of scene)

Act II, Scene IV

(At the inn where Jesus was born. Mary, Joseph, and Rhoda are there relaxing. They are breathing a sigh of relief. Mary and Joseph are first on stage.)

Joseph	Well, Mary, here we are. Free at last, safe forever. Our God has protected us.
Mary	What an escape! What an experience! What a scare! What a journey!
Joseph	We have certainly come a long way. Things have truly turned around for us.
Mary	The long days of panicking and hiding; the long nights of sleeping with our eyes opened; watching…worrying…wondering… whispering…waiting for relief. And now that time has finally come.
Joseph	You know, Mary, that is why it is so important for us to read and believe the scriptures. Do you remember how God protected our ancestors from the wicked hands of Pharaoh? It was long and exhausting for them. They faced the same kind of anxieties that we faced. But yet at the end, they were able to sing to the Lord for the horse and the rider were thrown into the waters. Pharaoh's chariots and his army were hurled into the sea.
Mary	Joseph, is it not amazing how God works? First, His people escape from Egypt. Now He allowed us to escape into Egypt.
Joseph	So no matter how bleak things may look, no matter how many darts are thrown at us, we are going to trust the Almighty God for the victory.

Mary	Just as our ancestor David did, we will trust Him. For The Lord is our shepherd so we will never be in want. So yea, though we walk through the valley of the shadow of death, we will fear no evil, for He is with us. His rod and His staff will comfort us.
Joseph	He prepared a table for us in the presence of our enemies. He anointest our heads with oil and our cup runneth over. Just imagine what a few passing months can do.
Mary	Surely goodness and mercy shall follow us all the days of our lives; And we shall dwell in the House of the Lord forevermore. *(Enter Rhoda and Lois. By now, Lois has had an epiphany in relation to the baby.)*
Rhoda	Mary, Joseph, the baby just smiled. His first smile…at least the first one that I saw, and He did so when Lois, of all persons, held Him in her hands.
Mary	My baby smiled? The Lord Jesus smiled!
Lois	It was so ironic. I did not know what to expect when I first held Him, but it was almost like He was saying… He was thinking, "You're forgiven." Joseph *(laughingly)* Lois. You are fine. You are not the only one to have had a conversion experience, and I am sure that there will be others to follow.
Lois	Joseph, you just said "just imagine what a few passing months can do." I look back now, and as I reflect, all I can remember is how cruel and horrible I was. Mean spirited, unbelieving, spiteful, and sometimes even hateful. But now that I have seen baby Jesus with my own eyes, now that I have met Him, my whole life has been changed. Believe me, I believe.

Rhoda

And that is why He came into the world. We have long expected the messiah and He has finally come. This world will be a better place. I even heard that people everywhere are getting really excited. The news has been spreading so fast.

Lois

Tell me about it! The shepherds did not waste any time after they encountered the angels. They shared the news with the other shepherds, and now the news has been spreading like wildfire.

Joseph

It only takes a spark to get a fire going, and soon all those around are warmed up by its glowing.

Mary

I feel so blessed. I feel so special to be the mother of the savior of the world.

Lois

And like the shepherds, my coworkers and I will be on a mission to spread the wonderful news. Tod, Sim, and even Japhat have also been converted, and like me, they feel so guilty about us been cold and callous at first when you wanted to stay here and have your baby. *(She sobs)* Now I do not want you to leave. I wish that you could stay here with us all year round.

Mary

You are so nice, Lois, but no, I cannot stay. My baby will be on a mission. As He grows and matures, He will be about His Father's business.

Lois

His Father's business? Do you mean that He will be a carpenter too?

Mary

Yes. He may become a carpenter, but there will be more to His life. Joseph here is His earthly father, but I am talking about the Heavenly Father. My baby has come to earth for a purpose.

Joseph

When the angel first appeared to me, He said that His name is to be called Jesus for He will save His people from their sin.

Rhoda

This is so sweet. I am grandmother to the savior of the world.

Mary	You are also blessed and have found favor in the sight of God. But I must go now. I want to go check upon Him. He must also be longing to see His Mama.
Mary	*(To Joseph)* Joseph, perhaps we should go and relieve Charlotte and Japheth. They have been spending a good part of the morning with Baby Jesus.
Joseph	You are right, Mary. Plus, to be honest, I am a little hungry too. I need to have my fill of something really good to eat.
Lois	Joseph, we have the best food at this inn. You will be always happy with whatever you choose to have.
Mary	Shall we go then, Joseph?
Joseph	Sure, Mary. Let us go *(they depart)*.
Lois	They are such a fine couple. God could not have made a better choice to become the earthly parents of Baby Jesus.
Rhoda	I know…and I do agree with you. *(There is the sound of a buzzer indicating that someone wants to come in. Lois goes to check it out. Prince Reuben and Princess Leah have found their way to see Baby Jesus. But Tod and Sim comes ahead of them to introduce them.)*
Lois	*(to Tod and Sim who are now on stage)* Oh, it is you two. How goes it, my friends?
Sim	Lois. It is unbelievable. How do people even know that Mary and Joseph and the baby are staying here? You are not going to believe who are waiting to see the little baby boy.
Rhoda	This sounds like a little more excitement is brewing. With whose presence are we now going to be further blessed?
Tod	I did not have a dream, but this feels like a dream to me. The royal prince and the royal princess are waiting to meet Baby Jesus.

Lois	Who? Are you kidding me? *(To Rhoda)* These are two comedians. You have got to take everything they say with a grain of salt.
Sim	But really, there is no salt this time. No Lois. We are not joking. Prince Reuben and Princess Leah are waiting in the wings. They are both very excited.
Rhoda	Goodness! Gracious! Me! Do you mean the offspring of King Herod? How did they get away?
Lois	I told you that this Baby Jesus is a game changer and a life changer. *(To audience)* Can you not all believe? Do you not all believe that Jesus can and will change lives? If He changed my life, He can certainly change your life as well.
Sim	And mine too!
Tod	He changed my life too! *(Enter Mary, Joseph, Leah, and Reuben; Joseph has the baby in his arms.)*
Rhoda	Mary, Joseph, you two need to get some rest. Why are you back in here so quickly? *(She sees Leah and Reuben)* So who are these? Oh, are these prince and princess royals? *(Embarrassingly)* I do not even know how to address you.
Tod	Prince Reuben and Princess Leah have both travelled all this way to meet Baby Jesus.
Mary	We met them in the hallway…it was sheer coincidence really…but they are both so charming.
Reuben	Thank you, everyone. I thank the Gods, whoever they are, that we have this privilege and honor.
Sim	No. We have the privilege and honor. You have come from the King's palace.
Leah	We have forfeited the rights to any earthly royalty. We wanted to see the newborn king. We just wanted to see Jesus.
Joseph	Oh, Glory be to God. What a wonderful change in our hearts this has been? Did everyone hear that? They have forfeited their rights to royalty.

Reuben	Yes, we have…so please drop the "prince" from Reuben.
Leah	And please drop the "princess" from Leah.
Sim	What…is…this?
Tod	Oh, My Lord. This is all such great fellowship, but I have to go and get some more work done. It has been my privilege to be a part of this company if you will excuse me. *(he exits)*
Lois	But Prince Reuben…
Reuben	You did not hear what I said? I am just Reuben.
Lois	Sorry, Leah and Reuben, what if King Herod sends the troops out in search of you and they find you here? That means we are in big trouble.
Leah	Please do not worry about that. That is never going to happen.
Lois	But how can you be so sure? Did you talk to him?
Reuben	Our dad is constantly in bed. He is seeing no one. He is eating no food. He is drinking no wine.
Leah	He has taken this so hard; it is as if the world is caving in on him.
Rhoda	Oh, that is so sad!
Tod	You're feeling sorry for him?
Rhoda	Well… I guess…
Sim	Oh, never mind! *(To Lois)* Lois, I think that I need to go and help Tod in his project. He has a deadline, and I feel obliged to help him. *(He exits)*
Reuben	*(to Rhoda)* Our dad will be fine. My mom is trying to cheer him on, but she is taking it hard too.
Leah	Just not as hard.
Lois	Lord, have mercy! So how did you get out of the palace? You must have run away.
Leah	We cannot tell you that. Now that is a royal secret, and if we tell, that is when some people may get into trouble

Mary	We do not want anyone to get into trouble. We are just glad that you have made it safely. I just hope that you will both be okay.
Reuben	*(jokingly)* We would both be okay if we could take the baby home with us. *(They all chuckle)*
Leah	The truth is that when our father started to get all angry and bent out of shape, we were seriously wishing that the baby could have become a part of our family.
Joseph	Not to worry, now we are all part of one big, happy family. Our God has sent His son into the world to unite us all and make us one.
Leah	*(to Joseph)* I thought that the baby was your son.
Joseph	He is my son, but God is His Heavenly Father.
Leah	This is so confusing!
Reuben	Leah, it does not matter who is the real father, so do not be confused. I am just happy that I can get to see Him. *(To Mary).* Can I hold Him in my arms?
Mary	How about if you wait a few years? When He grows healthy and strong, He is going to be so happy to meet and greet and spend time with everyone.
Reuben	But still, can we hold Him now?
Mary	I wish you could, but according to God's instructions, certain things need to be put in place first. There are a number of ceremonial practices that we need to adhere to before you can hold Him.
Reuben	Oh man!

Joseph	Oh yes, we need to have Him circumcised. So we will all need to take Him to the temple where He is to meet the old priest Simeon. God has revealed to Simeon that he will not die until he gets to see Jesus face to face. Maybe after Simeon holds Him and blesses Him, then others may get to hold Him too.
Leah	So who is this Simeon? How come he gets to hold the baby?
Reuben	Right. That's not fair! We were here first, we saw Him before Simeon will even get to see Him.
Mary	And that's how it is, Reuben. God has a plan. Some things may not appear to be fair to us, but God knows what He is doing.
Joseph	You see, this Simeon is a devout and righteous man whom God selected for a purpose. *(Tod enters)*
Tod	O-ho, o-ho, o-ho, o-ho. The gods are on our side. We have met another man of God, and what a joy it is for me to lead him in.
All On Stage	Man of God? Man of God?
Tod	Sim, will you come on in? And take him with you? *(All looks surprised and are speechless when Sim walks in with Simeon. There is a one-minute musical march to fill the gap, then Sim speaks.)*
Sim	And so here He is, the real man of God.
Simeon	*(voice cracking/vibrating reflecting his age)* I heard my name…and here I am.
Mary	Simeon, we were supposed to be coming to you, but you have come to us.
Simeon	And that is truly our God at work. He has come to us in the form of this little baby. And through Him, this whole world can be saved.
Joseph	I get it; I get it. He came to Mary through the angel; He came to me through the angel; He came to Zechariah and Elizabeth through an angel.

Lois	And do not forget; He came to me too and has changed my life completely.
Sim	And to me…
Tod	And to me…
Reuben	And to me and my sister
Leah	And to the whole world.
Rhoda	*(to audience)* God will come to you too if you will let Him
Simeon	So now let Him come to me too. We do not have to be at the temple. God is not confined to the four walls of the temple; He is outside the walls of the temple; He is everywhere.
Joseph	*(walking up to Mary)* Mary, Simeon is going to bless our son right here. Please let Him come to me so that He can go to Simeon. He has truly come to this world just as the prophets proclaimed. God is with us; He has come into this world in flesh. *(Walks over to Simeon and gives the baby to him. Simeon takes the baby.)*
Simeon	*(holding up the baby)* Sovereign Lord, as You have promised, let now your servant depart in peace. For my eyes have seen your salvation which you have prepared in the sight of all people, a light for revelation to the gentiles and for glory to your people, Israel…

(Curtain/End of Scene
End of Musical)
(Appropriate version of "The Hallelujah Chorus" is played or sung
after which players come out for the curtain call.)

THE FOLLOWING SCRIPT REPRESENTS AN OPTIONAL SET OF SCENES WHICH A DIRECTOR OR PRODUCER MAY CONSIDER USING AS ACT TWO. THE STORY LINE IS SIMILAR AND AS SUCH, SECTIONS FROM EACH OPTIONAL ACT MAY BE EXTRACTED FROM ONE AND USED IN THE OTHER OR, ALTERNATIVELY, DIRECTORS/PRODUCERS MAY USE THE ADDITIONAL OPTION BELOW IN PLACE OF THE ORIGINAL ACT TWO IN THE ORIGINAL SECTION OF THE MUSICAL.

OPTIONAL ACT TWO—SCENE ONE— OUTSIDE THE INN AND SEVERAL MONTHS HAVE PASSED BY

The innkeepers are having a meal together. Two are male and one is female. Their names are Tod, Sim, and Lois.

TOD	This is good meat, it ought to be like this every day. I would never think then of leaving this job.
SIM	Oh, I have had it more spicy. You need to visit Lois at home, and she will give you a taste of what really good meat is. Wouldn't you Lois?
LOIS	You see, Tod will find anything delicious. He is such a glutton. His compliment is certainly no recommendation.
SIM	He thinks highly of everything that passes the throat so long as it is not poisonous. That is some stomach he has there.
TOD	Never mind my stomach, I tell you. I see my physician every month and he thinks that I am in good shape.
LOIS	I Think that you are in good shape too but please do not spoil it by eating so much.
TOD	*(reaches over to help himself from Lois's plate).* You make sure to stay in shape my dear. I can help you do just that just right.
SIM	You cannot change. It is clear. One can never guess what might happen to you if there is a famine.

TOD	So I store up now in anticipation of that possibility *(reaches over and takes from Sim's plate too)*. You are the ones who need to worry because you will not have anything in store. *(A TALL FIGURE COMES AND PASSES THROUGH AND GIVES SOME INSTRUCTIONS. HE IS IN A SUPERVISORY ROLE.)*
MANAGER	Your mealtime will soon be up folks. As soon as you are done, you will need to come and see me so I can send you on a special assignment for the afternoon.
LOIS	Sir, it is so cold. It is so cold. We are freezing here and there seems to be no end to the admission of new guests. This does make our work a little harder.
MANAGER	That's what we are here for. Service. Service is how we make our money. That is how you get paid. You did not know this?
LOIS	Get paid? Get paid? We could really do without that which you have to offer. My purpose for coming here is to avoid boredom. I can hardly claim to have any real interest in my job.
SIM	You need to speak for yourself Lois *(To Manager)* Sir, the work is hard, but I do get fulfillment from serving. It is such a ....
TOD	Up and down! Round and round! So, the old story goes. When the work is up; I will. be up and when the work is down, I will be down. So, I am with it too even if it goes round and round.
MANAGER	Well, let me tell you why our beds are crammed. Ever since those two inns- the one across the grove and the smaller one up the road- were closed; you know in keeping with the emperor's Policies to close down as many inns as possible, people have been flocking this one because it is so difficult to find nearby ones. In one room – the one near the hall - people are virtually sleeping three in one bed!

LOIS	So, my body must wear, and my energy depleted because of one man? This is some fine we must pay for trying to stay alive!!!
MANAGER	This is the story of life, I guess. Now for your assignment. We are expecting some new beds and other furnishings later today. There will have to be a radical restructuring of all the fixtures here. I want to begin by asking you two men to have the west and south halls emptied. Pack all the equipment into the other two halls. Then we shall make temporary bed facilities so as to accommodate our new quota of furnishings.
TOD	Sir, that's a tall order!
SIM	We must do all that in one night?
MANAGER	Perhaps not in one night but if you can arrange to have it done by the morrow, your efforts will be commendable. The key to success is hard work, they say.
LOIS	Oh, some of us work hard but without success
MANAGER	Not you my dear Lois. Your thoughts are too negative. Gentlemen. Shall we have a go at it?
SIM	I'll be at it Sir.
TOD	We may not make it, but we will try.
MANAGER	Lois, this means that you may have to take care of all the visits for the rest of the day.
LOIS	*(Sarcastically)* I could tell you that was coming.
MANAGER	See if you work a little harder, you will succeed. It's in your hands now people. Our new rooms must be ready for opening in ten or twelve days. In the meantime, we cannot accept any new guests until this is done unless, of course, it is a real emergency.
TOD	The ideal thing to do would be to ask some of those who are not seriously ill to go home. This should help to provide some space.

SIM	Well, it would not be easy to do that. We are on contract. Are we not?
MANAGER	Sure. We cannot really send people home. At least, not so easily. It would be hard even to close the doors on new ones but there comes a time when the hearts have got to be hardened.
LOIS	So, the doors are closed. I understand and so they shall remain. *(Another figure appears. It is a man and his little daughter. His name is Eton)*
MANAGER	Yes Sir. Can we help you? What is your mission?
ETON	Ah; it is my little daughter here. She goes into periods of excitement and anxiety and this manifests itself in unbearable ways. There are times when she ....
MANAGER	If she must remain for treatment, you may have a problem Sir. We have run out of rooms. Anyway, this dear lady will take care of you. At least, she will try. She deals with this area of our hospitality. I am running off but I wish you luck. *(Lois, Sim, and Tod look up at him surprisingly and then look at each other. Lois has a disgusting look as he departs).*
LOIS	How could he? I mean......
TOD	It's shocking.
ETON	Well, are you going to attend to me?
LOIS	I wish I could.
ETON	But that's what I understand. Aren't you in charge?
SIM	She isn't really. He is. That gentleman who just left has all the authority.
ETON	Now somebody is hiding something from me!
LOIS	So, I will deal with you. Please tell me what you would want us to do with your little girl.
ETON	I cannot deal with her on my own. So that if we could have her examined thoroughly, then you might treat her afterwards. Would this be asking too much?

LOIS	The problem is that there are no beds for her to rest. They are all taken up with all manner of diseases and illnesses.
ETON	But Madam, there was already a standby arrangement for her to be put up. This was made weeks ago.
LOIS	I do not know who was responsible for this but regardless, this would have to be changed. This is simply impractical.
ETON	I could bring you a little folding bed for my daughter to rest on. I may even donate it to you afterwards, but she has to be seen. *(There is no reply)* ......Can this work? *(Still no reply)* ......Did you hear me? ....how about that?........could you find room?
SIM	Sir, you may want to stop trying now. She is a hard task master.
ETON	At this rate, we may soon run out of rooms in the cemetery. People will just keep dying.
LOIS	It's too bad!!
ETON	*(GRABBING HIS DAUGHTER BY THE HAND AND PULLING HER HARD)* Come little one, there are no human beings in this place. Let me take you home to die. *(HE DEPARTS. ALL THREE LOOK AT EACH OTHER.)*
LOIS	So, we are beasts. That's what we have been reduced to. Whoever comes next will suffer for that.
TOD	Our manager goofed. He should be made to pay for this.
SIM	He stays behind and makes all the rules. Then he sends us forward to do all the dirty work.
LOIS	Well, I will not be doing any more of it. I shall leave this chair unmanned. All of Bethlehem could come and take over if they want. *(Sarcastically);* I am a beast.
SIM	Lois!

LOIS	What?
SIM	You can't do that
LOIS	Then you will see.
TOD	Unless we find that noticeboard which we use to inform people that all the rooms have been taken up.
SIM	Which notice board is that?
TOD	Oh, you are too new here Sim. There is a sign somewhere here with the words marked on it......I think.... or.....yes simply, "Sorry, All rooms occupied."
SIM	Oh Yes. I have seen it around the place. I think that I may even know where to find it. Let me go and get it. *(HE LEAVES)*.
TOD	You know Lois. I think I know how you feel. Nobody will think anything ill of our manager for he is not upfront to face patrons. We will get all the blame and we are going to be seen as the worst creatures ever to walk upon the face of the earth.
LOIS	What a coward he is? He played a nasty trick on me but before this day is done, he'll be the victim and I will be the victor. I am going to play it back on him. *(SIM BRINGS OUT SIGN AND BEGINS TO HAND IT TO LOIS)*. Don't give it to me. Just put it up where everyone can see. We are all doing this together.
SIM	Here Tod, please give me a hand. *(TOD GOES ACROSS. TOGETHER THEY PUT UP THE SIGN FOR ALL TO SEE)*. How about that? Half the work is done.
LOIS	Half the work is done? The whole work is done. This notice will talk to others. I shall be behind doors just like Mr. manager. Are you coming fellows?
SIM	Most certainly, we are.
TOD	Protest? Okay Let's go. *(THEY DEPART)*

THE GROUP/COMPANY COMES OUT AND DOES CHORAL
SPEAKING VERSE.

> Full of anger, bitterness, and hate
> All three did leave an unmanned gate.
> Determined they would stay away.
> From all that people had to say.
> Now time went by, - two hours or three -
> And still, no one that people could see.
> Till Joseph and Mary reached that same gate
> And for attention, they patiently wait.

(ENTER JOSEPH AND MARY)

MARY	Are we there now? What a long journey? This is such an awful feeling.
JOSEPH	This is the one I am sure, but no one seems to be there.
MARY	So, knock or shout or something. We must get attention soon.
JOSEPH	Ya-ho; Ya-ho! *(HE KNOCKS)*. How irresponsible is it to leave the gate unmanned? Ya-ho! Perhaps I should go further inside and see if we are at the right place.
MARY	No. I do not want to be left outside Joseph; This a strange place and so it would be dangerous. *(SHE LOOKS UP AND SEES THE SIGN; THEN SPEAKS WITH ANXIETY IN HER VOICE)* Look Joseph, look!
JOSEPH	What now sweetie?
MARY	*(POINTING TO THE SIGN)* Is This our luck or am I interpreting incorrectly?
JOSEPH	Wrong interpretation; I am sure.... I think......at least, I hope. This could not happen in a public inn. It is the only one in the entire township.
MARY	So, we may be in the wrong place. Joseph, I would not be able to go another inch if this journey

continued. Please do something to make this the right place.

JOSEPH	I am trying my best. Mary, you would not have to worry. Yours is a special case and so they will understand. To give birth is life or death and so they must give you special attention. They would be extremely sympathetic to a case such as this and so even if they were full, they would certainly make room for you. What is more, you are going to be the mother of the Savior of the world. If only the innkeeper knew this, he would have been here waiting for us instead of us waiting for him.

What a privilege and what an honor the management of this inn will experience when many years from this day, they will be able to report that the savior of the world was born here. |
MARY	You make it sound so exciting. I feel quite consoled. But why would they put this notice up? No one may come to see us for the rest of the day!!
JOSEPH	Well, I must go and find someone. They are human beings like us who work here Mary. They feel pain and experience anxiety. They experience stress, sorrow, and sadness just like we do. It is an inn, so they care for those who need help. Okay? So let us just patiently wait. Let us show some faith and believe that God is going to be with you until I get back; but I must find the assistance which we need. *(HE TURNS TO GO THROUGH ONE DOOR AND SIM PASSES THROUGH BEHIND HIM).*
SIM	Sir, you cannot go through there. Do you need something?
JOSEPH	I am Sorry. It is just that we were waiting for such a long time, and we got no attention so I thought that I would go in search of someone to help us. Then God sent you along.
SIM	God sent you along? What kind of help do you need then?

JOSEPH	My name is Joseph, and this is my wife...... this is Mary. We need to be placed in a room so that.......
SIM	*(POINTING TO NOTICE SIGN)*. See brother, that says it all.
MARY	I am going to have a baby. *(HOLDS HER BELLY)*. Can't you see?
SIM	That would hardly make a room available automatically!
JOSEPH	Could it really be that in a public inn, you have run out of room to accommodate people who need your services?
SIM	That is what the notice is saying. Exactly that.
JOSEPH	And What will people do? I have never heard of this in any other town or country.
SIM	Actually, this was a recent decision for this inn. We seem to set the standard for good or for evil.
MARY	But you would bend your rules for one in my condition, I am sure. Listen sir, I am tired and worn out. I shall die if I were not allowed in.
SIM	Even in your condition, NO! Well........you know what? At least, I could try but I could not make you any commitment or give you any promises.
JOSEPH	*(EXCITEDLY)* What can you do? You can see that she is in a plight.
SIM	I shall go and check with the woman who would normally make the appointments and bookings. I shall be back in a little while.
JOSEPH	Thank You. We shall wait *(SIM EXITS; THEN SPEAKS TO MARY)* If it is a woman, then surely, she would be sympathetic to your case.
MARY	I was so glad when I heard him say 'woman'. *(HOLDS HER SIDE)*. This pain sticks like a needle. Lord, please let him return quickly.
JOSEPH	My life is in God. He placed us in this situation. He shall surely lead us out. *(SIM RETURNS WITH LOIS)*.

SIM	Here they are. Joe.........something.
JOSEPH	Joseph is my name, and this is my wife, Mary.
LOIS	Are you able to read Sir?
JOSEPH	Yes. I think that I can. I have seen your notice but.......
LOIS	There are no 'buts' *(POINTING TO NOTICE)*. And do you speak and understand that language?
JOSEPH	I do but if only you would give me an ear!
LOIS	That's all I'll be able to give you. An ear. For as you can see, we can offer no help.
MARY	I do not believe this.
LOIS	Life is full of shocks and surprises. In this world, you will find much more unbelievable.
SIM	I shall have to leave. I cannot take this *(EXITS)*
MARY	I am going to have a child. I must get some help.
LOIS	So, I know. I wish that I could help.
JOSEPH	Lady, we have been traveling for miles and breathed a sigh of relief when we got here. We can hardly go any further. Is there anything you could possibly do to help?
LOIS	N- O. I can only suggest that since your dear wife is so heavy with child, that you pick up your feet and continue for the next set of miles before she collapses. I do hope that will help.
MARY	What inhumanity? I have never seen this!
LOIS	Neither have I. I am so sorry, but I do not have a lot of time left. I would like to go back to my task inside. Do you mind? *(SHE POINTS TO SIGN AGAIN)*. All...rooms....occupied!!!!!!! (SHE TURNS TO LEAVE).
JOSEPH	Goodness. Are you woman or are you beast? *(ANGRILY)* Do you feel? Do you know? Have you emotions? Is there sympathy within you? Do you have a heart? Is this the best you can do for someone whose life you can save? *(BURSTING INTO TEARS)*

Is there someone around here who is human enough to understand?

MARY

(BEGINNING TO CRY AS WELL). Joseph. Do not get angry. Remember that The Lord is on our side. If I give birth to my son on the road, I'll say, this is how He wants it to be.

LOIS

Am I woman or am I beast? Be off with you *(ANGRILY TOO).* I have been given authority here, so you listen when I speak. We are not going to save you nor your wife, or anyone else. There just isn't room. Do you understand?

No room.

JOSEPH

(Calmer) It is as simple as that. You are not human enough to understand that by helping and making an effort, you can save a life. If you only knew the future of Him who is to be born, you would give up your own room. *(MANAGER ENTERS. HE WAS ATTRACTED BY THE SHOUTING AND YELLING).*

MANAGER

This is disgraceful stuff. Why is all this taking place?

Joseph

Real disgraceful. This inn is...........

LOIS

(ADDRESSING INNKEEPER). You are the reason it is taking place. You are the one who decided we could not take in anymore guests or patients. So now, I must put up with.... put up with....... Now I must put up with......*(LOOKS AT JOSEPH)* all and sundry. I have to face the public to tell them 'No room'. While you get away without insults being hurled at you. You have not been called an animal; You have not been told that you have no heart; nor feelings ......nor concern for anyone......but I have. *(TO JOSEPH)* Let me answer your question sir. Am I woman or am I beast? I am woman but *(POINTING TO MANAGER)* ......here is the beast.

MANAGER

What is all this in aid of? What is happening?

LOIS	You make the rules, so you tell them what is happening. We do not have space for anyone else. Do we?
MANAGER	*(TO JOSEPH AND MARY)*. Whatever she tells you, you will have to go by. I cannot do anything.
JOSEPH	You need to know the importance of this birth. Mary is going to give birth to the savior of the world.
MANAGER	What Savior? Of what world?
JOSEPH	the baby will grow up to be the savior of the entire world.
LOIS	What is a savior. May I ask?
JOSEPH	Do you not know the scriptures? We all need to be saved from sin and ....
LLIS	Oh. Never mind. I don't think that I will ever understand.
MANAGER	Is this going to be somebody important then?
JOSEPH	Very Much So. That's why you should make room for His birth.
MANAGER	So sad but I am not convinced. If I am to be sorry later, then so be it.
JOSEPH	And you will *(IN PRAYER)* Lord!! Help us. *(JOSEPH TAKES MARY BY THE HAND AND THEY TURN TO DEPART)*.
LOIS	Cheerio. There is a place That's not so good down the road. You may want to try that. You come to this side and I will tell you how to get there.
JOSEPH	Come on Mary. Let's go. Our God will provide. *(THEY TURN AND SING TOGETHER "THOU DIDST LEAVE THY THRONE AND THY KINGLY CROWN"- VERSES ONE AND THREE. THE LIGHTS FADE AS THE COMPANY CONTINUES THE STORY IN VERSE.)*

No room they say in their inn.
Once more the process must begin.
Of searching, seeking, longing, waiting
To see the son of God appearing
So, on their way, they both did go.
Sometimes they're high; sometimes they're low.
To try and find a lovely bed.
For baby Jesus to lay His head.

Now after traveling on and on
To give birth to their first-born son
They came upon the chosen place.
Where they would look upon His face
Hey! We shall have to change the scene.
And move from where we have just been.
No longer with those hearts so hard
But in a filthy, dirty yard.

(BY NOW THE STAGE IS RESET FOR MANGER SCENE WHICH OPENS WITH JOSEPH AND MARY SPEAKING WITH THE KEEPER OF THE STABLE. HIS NAME IS JAPHAT)..

JAPHAT	Over this side Sir, right over here. Let us move quickly so as not to cause any delay.
JOSEPH	This is most kind of you. We were wondering when we were going to get some help.
JAPHAT	Oh, I have been expecting you. God revealed to me that He wanted me to assist in making the arrangements for your wife right here. Is she alright though?
MARY	Not doing too badly but we must find somewhere for me to give birth to my child and get some rest. This pain is too much for me.
JAPHAT	The main place which I had in mind is to be ready shortly. I should hope that we can extend our patience a bit until it is ready.

MARY	Patience we have but nature's process may not have much regard for effort no matter how genuine.
JOSEPH	We must proceed to the room now if we can please.
JAPHAT	But there is no point. It is just being cleaned now.
JOSEPH	But we were directed here. I thought that it would all be ready. Do you mean that we are in for another disappointment?
JAPHAT	I sincerely hope not. We are trying our best.
MARY	And What shall we do then with this emergency?
JAPHAT	If you did not want to wait until the place........
JOSEPH	You mean there is somewhere else?
JAPHAT	Not really. Well, yes.........I could think of another option but *(SMILING EMBARRASSINGLY)* ....you would not be interested in that surely.
MARY	Sir. Anything will do right now. Just anywhere. There is more than a degree of urgency.
JAPHAT	How could I allow you to experience discomfort? I am not even sure how clean it is.
JOSEPH	If you understand what an emergency is then......
JAPHAT	Okay then. *(POINTS TOWARDS AN AREA)*. Over there is fairly new and it has a newly built stable attached. *(LOOKS DOWN THEN AFTER A PAUSE, LOOKS UP ON JOSEPH)*.
JOSEPH	Go on. I am hearing you.
JAPHAT	Do you think that a stable would be okay? *(CHOKING ON HIS WORD)*
JOSEPH	What for? To do what?
JAPHAT	We're talking about staying for a day or two and having a child. Right?
JOSEPH	Right But.......so what?
JAPHAT	So, I am saying that if you are in a desperate rush, and you care to, then we could have you use the inner

section of the stable. It might not be so comfortable but that is the best that there is in a state of emergency.

MARY

You're not serious sir?

JAPHAT

Yet... I am not laughing. There is not even the thought of a smile in my mind. *(MARY AND JOSEPH GLANCE AT EACH OTHER).*

JOSEPH

This is not our day. Come Mary, we may as well go out into the street. Let's go into any public area.

JAPHAT

You will find this place nice and peaceful and quiet. There is a gust of fresh air which passes through continuously and it is extremely private.

MARY

It would be an insult to God if after having given me the honor of being the mother of the Savior of the world for me to make His place of birth a stable. It seems quite wrong.

JOSEPH

Just the thought of it is a bit discomforting and maybe offensive. the son of man? The son of God?

JAPHAT

I suppose you can make your choice. You may find a better place. The big question is when that shall be. When I first heard of your situation, I thought that I would be nice and try to be helpful. I would really love for you to have the nicest atmosphere but within the context of your own urgency, the easiest thing is what you find offensive. However, I figured you might have found it uncomfortable and that is why I was even hesitant to mention this as a possibility. You have stated your case well. It is quite clear and therefore understood. Whatever is the will of God in this situation, will surely come to pass. Good luck in your thinking.

MARY

Joseph, is it possible for us to go to see the stable before we make a decision? Might this not also be in the will of God?

JOSEPH
I am prepared to go see it, but I hardly think that we will find it acceptable. Do you see yourself lying with oxen and horses and sleeping through that noise and that smell? How could you rest amidst bellowing and mooing and bleating all at once? Impossible.

MARY
Still dear. God's will must be done. JAPHAT, if you will take us there, we will examine your stable. I have really had enough tension and anxieties.

JAPHAT
At your service, therefore. What an honor it would be for me to know that I played a part in this great miracle? Let us use this exit. Shall we? *(MARY AND JOSPEH SINGS)*

WE'RE NOT ALONE
We're not alone amidst our grief.
Our God shall bring us sweet relief.
When in our hands shall lay our boy
Our sadness will be turned to joy.
No one will put up with a stranger.
Our Lord's birthplace shall be a manger.

Chorus We know the Father will have His way.
Help us always your word to obey!

We thank you Lord that You will give.
The son of Man on earth to live.
You want us to His parents be.
It's one big task as you can see.
As we have listened to your message
May we still show we are in your image.

And so, as we prepare to go.
To take off this, our earthly woe
We humbly ask you, guide our mind.
That we will then the right place find

Then help us to accept your blessing.
With thankful hearts and tongues confessing

That you O Father will have your way
Help us always your word to obey.

*COMPANY SINGS FIRST TWO VERSES
OF "AWAY IN A MANGER"*

CURTAIN.

ACT TWO, SCENE TWO
(HEROD'S PALACE)

Christ is born - Oh yes, He's born.
Is He born? Of course, He's born.
Born- A mean and lowly birth.
Born - A Savior on this earth.
Hallelujah - Praise the Lord
Praise The Lord - O Let us thank Him.
Christ is in the manger sleeping.
Men who were their sheep a-keeping
Went to praise their newborn King.
Whose birth men and angels sing.

Christ is born - He is The Lord
So, let us join in one accord.
To tell it with the loudest note
Can't speak low, we'll have to shout.
Hallelujah- Praise the Lord
Praise The Lord - Oh Let us thank Him.
Kings shall on their throne be mourning.

Gifts to Christ will just be pouring.
Shout it from the mountain top!
From the valley - Let's not stop
Christ is born; is born; is born.
Jesus. Christ is born.

(COMPANY SINGS "GO TELL IT ON THE MOUNTAIN". THIS IS FOLLOWED BY TWO PERSONS DANCING TO "JOY TO THE WORLD" (SLOWER VERSION)); AT THE END OF WHICH BOTH PERSONS OPEN CURTAIN FOR DRAMA. HEROD IS SEATED ON HIS THRONE WITH A LOOK OF DISMAY ON HIS FACE. PRISCILLA, THE QUEEN IS WITH HIM.)

HEROD	I feel so threatened, I wish that I was never born.
PRISCILLA	You be calm now your majesty. Just try to be calm and let's watch the developments.
HEROD	I am prepared to watch all night but it is a bag of nerves speaking to you right now. Just the thought of losing my place on the throne.
PRISCILLA	Oh, for heaven's sake, think positively. Why should you think of the worst? You are only a few years on the throne. As far as I can see, your rule has been excellent. You have the people with you. You did so much which your father and grandfather before you were unable to do. Why do you think that your days of ruling would soon be over? Be off the negatives now. Please!!
HEROD	How I wish that I could be as confident as you are Lady Priscilla. Yet the reports which I have been getting indicate that the baby king of which they speak is not of the line of David. Well, I don't know.......wherever he is from, he is not a real king.

PRISCILLA	Even more reason why you should be calm. If he is a false king; even a puppet, there is no cause for alarm.
HEROD	That's precisely what makes it hard to accept. The fact that my people would want to give the real for the unreal, sincerity for falsehood. It is as if......you know......the burden of all who went before me is falling on my shoulder. I am carrying the sins of Ahab, Jehu, Solomon, Rehoboam, and others. The Fathers have eaten sour grapes, but my teeth are set on edge.
HEROD	Oh, Your Majesty! Your Majesty! Why should you be restless? What you have heard are but sketches of information from stray sources. There is nothing factual - at least, not yet- Not until these things are proven and they will never be.
HEROD	I shall know as soon as my attendants return. They have all gone on a mission to ascertain exactly what is happening down in Judea... I shall be most relieved when they return. I just hope that they will bring the news which I want to hear.
PRISCILLA	And if they don't, what? You won't sit here and pine all day. You cannot afford to let your attendants think that you are a coward - even if in fact, you are one. You are the king, and you will need to at least let them continue to see you as such; and remember now that you are the real king.
HEROD	I remember. *(HE TRIES TO CULTIVATE BOLDNESS BUT IT IS FAKE)* I am the real king. I am not a coward. I am not nervous, not in the least.
PRISCILLA	So stand like a king and show your worth. You are the sole authority here. Do you understand that clearly?

HEROD	*(STANDING UP AND AGAIN, MOMENTARILY SHOWING SOME STRENGTH)* I remember. I am the real king. How about this? See, I can stand. *(THEN IN A SUBDUED VOICE)* I only wish that I did not have all this burden to carry amidst all the other problems which we have in the palace. I could do with one less and this is the one which I would first want to eliminate.
PRISCILLA	Goodness! No use trying to keep you calm. You'd better give me that scepter and let me rule. You are obviously prepared to stay in the background and be dictated to by all those who are below you.
HEROD	That's not exactly the case Lady Priscilla. I....... *(ENTER TWO ATTENDANTS. THEY HAVE BROUGHT NEWS BACK FOR THE KING)*. Oh, here they come; Let me read their faces! The news is good; No, it is bad! I'm sure it is either good or bad.
FIRST ATTENDANT	His Majesty Sir; Her Majesty Madam. We sent with great haste as you instructed..........
HEROD	Don't tell me please! Don't tell me! No!
FIRST ATTENDANT	Your Majesty, there is much to hear. Too much to bear. I cannot bear it all unless you share it with me.
HEROD	So, keep it to yourself or take the queen aside and tell her secretly. I have enough burdens to bear without your additional ones.
PRISCILLA	I will have none of it either. If it's good, then tell it. If it's bad, then tell it to the king.
SECOND ATTENDANT	*(SPEAKING IN RHYTHMIC STYLE)*

There is not much time to pass the scepter from one hand to another.
Whoever rules must truly rule forever.
If now is not the time to hear what's there to tell
Then when tomorrow comes - as sure it must- it will not be well

Now is the time to fight the war if war is what there will be.
There's hardly time to knit your brow, O King listen to me.

(CONTINUING IN RHYTHMIC STYLE)

HEROD   I have seen it all

I close my eyes and see my mind O wandering away.
I see a lengthy night ahead that will not turn to day.
I see my throne all broken up and dashed in many pieces.
And in my heart, I see no end to pain that it releases.
Oh, if I could be born again, I would not want to be king.

SECOND   *(ALSO IN RHYTHMIC STYLE)*
ATTENDANT

Then shall I speak, or shall I not tell all that I have found?
How the angel of the Lord came down and glory shone around.
the many many shepherds who gathered one cold night.
And as they looked o'er all their sheep. They saw a light so bright.

PRISCILLA   *(RHYTHMIC STYLE CONTINUES)*

Ah, since you have begun this news which keeps us in suspense.
The only thing to do I think is listen with good sense.
Hold nothing back; forget no single word!
give an account of all you've gleaned!
Your voice will now be heard.

FIRST   And so, I will. I got my news first from those men
ATTENDANT   who heard it first. They were ordinary men and most
                                 unlearned, but it seems to be quite real.

HEROD   And who were these men? And what did they hear?

*(ATTENDANTS SING MEDLEY OF "THE FIRST
NOEL" VERSES 1&2; AND "WHILE SHEPHERDS
WATCHED THEIR FLOCK BY NIGHT" VERSES 1-4)*

HEROD	Did you hear anything about him being a king? That's the news which I dread the most.
SECOND ATTENDANT	Yes. Most certainly your majesty. The angels who brought the news, kept chanting a chorus *(SINGS CHORUS "COME AND WORSHIP; WORSHIP CHRIST THE NEWBORN KING)*. Sir, the streets of Bethlehem are full. Thousands of curious onlookers are converging on this small Judean Town.
PRISCILLA	But What for? What is so exciting?
FIRST ATTENDANT	Several feel that this is a prophecy being fulfilled. Something like a messiah or a survivor is what they call Him. He is supposed to be the one who will redeem Israel.......
SECOND ATTENDANT	Not a survivor, A Savior. That's who He is. He shall save this world from sin. So, they have called Him Jesus.
SECOND ATTENDANT	But He has another name......Ah......Emanuel. This means "God with us". His coming has brought God in direct contact with man. In fact, some even say that He is God!!
PRISCILLA	It all sounds quite blasphemous
HEROD	If the people believe it, it does not matter the degree of blasphemy which there might be. Blasphemy is a problem for the religious fanatics to deal with. Treason is what I am concerned about. What if all those who have gone along to Bethlehem all become convinced that this infant is King; then they may converge on my kingdom and try to dethrone me. I may have to tighten my security. I shall strengthen my army by thousands. The thought of losing my throne to an infant king is quite depressing.

PRISCILLA — Then kill all the infants in the land. Children and Youth. We will still have a land of adults - twenty and over.

HEROD — What a mammoth task that would be? It is a job that can hardly be accomplished. Try as hard as you might, there are so many Innocent lives that would be lost. This would be crazy and cruel.

PRISCILLA — My concern is not over those who are innocent; Too bad for them. My concern is for Him who is guilty. If He is slain among the infants, the job will be done.

FIRST ATTENDANT — Your Majesty Madam. This may be so but the task of killing all those under twenty years old would ruin the most promising sector of our country. And would this not also include our dear prince and charming princess?

PRISCILLA — Of course not! The royal blood shall not be touched. Neither by man nor by God.

SECOND ATTENDANT — Actually, there is no need to slay all of these. This child has been born for just a few weeks. To kill a twenty-year-old would certainly be missing the mark. Why don't we aim at an age group that is much younger?........say five years or thereabouts. The child can hardly grow beyond that even if the imagination is stretched to its limits.

HEROD — This still sounds like mass murder to me which is highly unnecessary.

PRISCILLA — Highly unnecessary? Well stay here and pine dear king about losing your throne. What brilliant suggestion do you have to offer to save your kingdom? Your blood might well be taken unless you first take blood.

FIRST ATTENDANT — May we consider therefore lowering our range to two years? If you make the decree your majesty, I shall enforce it first thing tomorrow. All the infants who are two years and under shall be slain.

PRISCILLA	How about that as a compromise Mr. King? Do you still call that unnecessary mass murder? Herod?
HEROD	It need not be all. That infant is male. Is he not?
FIRST ATTENDANT	He is your majesty.
HEROD	Very Well then. We shall slay only those who are male. I am totally for blood. Let the blood flow like the Nile. Every male child from Nazareth to Bethlehem. Let the sword pierce their side. Leave none untouched. For if you do, the one we want dead may remain alive.
PRISCILLA	You speak now like a man who is king and that is just how it is supposed to be. I will be behind you in this decree. After all, my place on the throne is lost if you are dethroned. The luxurious life which I now enjoy should not be traded for mere sympathy. Give me a heart that is too soft, and I will hand it right back to you again. I want a king who is able to rule with an iron heart. You make that decree, and I am with you forever. If you back out, it will only be the beginning of the end of your rule.
HEROD	My mind's made up. I see them dead. That infant king shall be no more. Gather all the swords and place them in thousands. Send out all the chariots by the hundreds.
SECOND ATTENDANT	Is this to commence now?
HEROD	Without delay. The king has spoken and when he speaks then you must carry out his word for whosoever does not, shall fall on his sword. Go get the word out as I have said.
PRISCILLA	Go on men. Do not allow him to have a change of heart.

ATTENDANTS	At your word your majesty Madam. Your majesty sir, your word will be carried out with haste. *(TWO ATTENDANTS DEPART)*.
HEROD	Lady Priscilla. There is still a dreaded fear within me.
PRISCILLA	Please do not start this all over again. I am going to break.
HEROD	It will be no good if they slay ten thousand babies and leave the king behind.
PRISCILLA	are you admitting that there is a king then?
HEROD	Other than he who is speaking now?
PRISCILLA	The reference would hardly be to you if you are beginning to have doubts again.
HEROD	Did It not bother you that so many persons were going to see the baby? In fact, not only to see Him but to worship Him. People have never sought to worship me. They never sing my praises. Yet He is but an infant.
PRISCILLA	Unless this a sign from the gods. But what would be the implications for our dynasty?
HEROD	I am thinking Lady Priscilla that I need to find this infant king Myself. I will have to go and see Him.
PRISCILLA	Whatever for? Are you going to join in worshipping Him also?
HEROD	Crazy! Crazy! I have no such thoughts. .... but I may very well have to go under that guise.
PRISCILLA	What would be your point? What would you hope to achieve?
HEROD	I simply want to mark His face. I'll have a part of my army with me. Then they will do battle.

PRISCILLA

It would appear to be quite strange. You are the king. The people know you wherever you go. How could you hail the birth of a so-called king that may be a threat to your throne especially when you are a king yourself? You are defeating yourself, your majesty.

HEROD

Then I shall not dress as king. I will have to hide my identity. Is that possible? Remove my royal gown; put down my scepter; forget my crown; put on my sandals; speak like a foreigner. That should do it. My own people will not know me. How do you feel?

PRISCILLA

I shall go with you. You shall not leave me behind. If there is a way to become unknown, I shall try it too. But how do we find the way?

HEROD

There is this story about some star which was supposed to have led the way. If we can find it........ *(FIRST ATTENDANT ENTERS AND HEROD ADDRESSES HIM)* Are they all dead?

FIRST ATTENDANT

Not yet your majesty but the word has gone out. The men are out in great numbers.

HEROD

I shall go to Bethlehem too.

FIRST ATTENDANT

Your Majesty. You do not have to. It has all been arranged.

HEROD

I want to make doubly sure that the child gets killed. I have that all arranged. I shall find the way with our delay. I'll let the world see that I am king.

FIRST ATTENDANT

It will not be easy, your majesty. Bethlehem 's a long way.

HEROD

And so, my friend., I give you three days to find three men. They will search especially for this child. Let them search extremely thoroughly. Let them search well. When they have found Him, let them come back to me and bring me word so that I may go and worship Him also.

FIRST ATTENDANT	Worship?
HEROD	Yes. Worship.........then death.

(HEROD ENGAGES IN VERSE SPEAKING)

I shall get Him, heaven knows.
Little man with big intent
All His friends may be my foes.
Yet I go; will not relent.
Take His life with my own knife!
So later on, there'll be no strife.

I shall get Him, there's no joke.
Dare Him think about my throne!
He shall bear a heavy yoke.
Instead of wearing any crown
Put Him out with all my might!
I don't have time for a fight.

I shall get Him, He's no king.
Several lives. may be destroyed.
I can't wait till it's morning.
This news makes me quite annoyed.

I shall search the whole world through.
Get His Mom and Papa too.

CURTAIN

ACT TWO, SCENE THREE
(THE HOME OF JOSEPH)

(MARY IS SITTING AND ROCKING WHILE HUMMING A TUNE. JOSEPH RUNS IN WITH EXCITEMENT BUT IS CLEARLY PANICKING.)

Joseph	Mary, Mary! Did you hear the news? I had another dream. Oh My God!! *(BREAKS DOWN IN TEARS)* Oh My God!!
MARY	*(CRYING TOO)*. What now Joseph? What news?
JOSEPH	It is about Herod. That wicked king!!
MARY	Herod?
JOSEPH	He has sent out orders that every male child who are two years old and under should be slain. Everyone without exception......and this would include our little boy Jesus.
MARY	Joseph, this cannot be true-not after all the trauma; not after all the pain; not after all the anxiety. He wouldn't come as far as Bethlehem. Would he?
JOSEPH	Yes, he would and even further. But The Lord is on our side. Hence the angel told me to flee. He suggested that I should take you and the baby and get down to Egypt with haste. He has assured me of His protection and guidance always.
MARY	Then why did you scream?

JOSEPH	I must have been quite at ease during all this. It was not until I started to get awake that my imagination ran wild, and I saw men chasing us on our way to Egypt.
MARY	Oh, the thought! *(IN DEEP DISTRESS)* The very thought. But if this is to be so Joseph, we ought not to wait. Should we not go now?
JOSEPH	By all means. I understand that even Herod himself is on his way. He is coming specially to mark out our son. But how can we leave now? Our parents are on their way to be with us. They will never find us if we leave now. The other problem is that we cannot even leave a note as this may fall into the wrong hands.
MARY	Not to mention good old Simeon. That poor old man who now waits for the consolation of Israel. I understand that even he is on his way to see us. Joseph, did you know that Simeon does not expect to die until his eyes behold baby Jesus?
JOSEPH	Except that it could be the will of God. You see, Simeon's hope is not merely a human wish or desire. It is the Divine will of God. Since this is so, we can allow time for Simeon to come and see our son. Our God would spear both Simeon and Jesus. They can look each other in the face.
JOSEPH	So, you spoke well Mary. Our trust will be in Him who first started the process of miracles.

(THREE MEN KNOCK AND ENTER WITHOUT WAITING FOR AN ANSWER. THEY SEEM PRETTY ANXIOUS. THEY ARE THE TRHEE MEN WHO CAME FROM HEROD.)

MARY	Oh God have mercy! Have mercy Oh God!
JOSEPH	Now who are you? From whom have you come? Herod, I guess.
FIRST MAN	Guessed right. He sent us here.

MARY	Oh no! Don't!!!
SECOND MAN	Do not scream or raise an alarm. We shall do no harm. Truly.
JOSEPH	You cannot afford to kill this child. He is the holy one of God. Born to save mankind from sin. If He perishes, then all of Israel perish. Perish forever. He is here for a purpose. He must remain alive.
THIRD MAN	He will remain alive, but we must see Him. We cannot leave until we see the infant King. We have come to worship Him.
MARY	If only I could trust your word.
SECOND Man	Please Do. See we have no swords; our hands are clean; our sides defenseless; our hearts are pure; our word is good.
JOSEPH	Oh God in heaven, if these men have evil in their hearts, then weaken their bones and let them faint. By your power and through Spirit, give us strength to conquer all. If their heart is as pure as gold, then let them remain strong. May you show us now that you protect your own. Speak to me Lord that even as I open mine eyes and look upon their faces, I will receive an answer. If they are flat on their faces, I'll know that they came to deceive. If they are standing on their feet, then my son they will receive. Hear me my God and answer my cry as my plea goes up to Thee.
FIRST MAN	So, we are still on our feet. Do you believe it now?
JOSEPH	Believe me, I believe. Mary, let us bring our son so these men may do Him whatever homage they may choose.
MARY	If you accept my darling, then so do I. *(SHE REACHES OVER AND IN A MINUTE, SHE TAKES HER BABY OUT, PUSHING HIM IN A ROLLING CRIB.)* This is What our little boy looks like. He is so sweet. Isn't He a charm?

THIRD MAN	*(STANDING OVER WITH OTHER TWO MEN AS THEY LOOK AT THE BABY)*. I think that He really is cute. Now you will see just why we are here and how we got here. *(ALL THREE MEN SING" WE THREE KINGS")*
MARY	Thank You sirs. I see that your hearts are truly pure. We were so afraid as we thought that Herod had sent you to kill our baby.
FIRST MAN	He did but we could never do that. Some voice spoke with us while we were on our way and told us quite clearly that this was wrong.
SECOND MAN	He just wanted to know what really to believe. He heard so much about the infant King and wanted to hear all the details so that he would know whether the child would turn out to be a threat to his throne or not.
THIRD MAN	Herod wanted us to seek out the child and asked that we bring word back to him.
JOSEPH	Bring word back to him? What word?
THIRD MAN	In fact, he claimed that he was coming to worship Him but that was not quite true. He merely wanted to do the killing himself. He bears a grudge that is as cruel as cruel can be.
MARY	Well, what are you going to tell him when you get back to him? It will be hard to say that you did not find us since you really did.
FIRST MAN	Oh, we do not have to go back. In fact, we do not plan to go back to him. He is so cruel; he may choose to kill even us.
JOSEPH	Your lives will be at stake; I am sure.
SECOND MAN	One's life is always in danger under Herod. You'll never know whether or not you will live through any day when he gives his commands. It really is wise that we run away.
JOSEPH	We started ....*(PAUSES)* to plan on running. We are going to Egypt. He would never find us there.

THIRD MAN	As fast as you can brother. Gallop with your wife and child.
JOSEPH	Oh, so we shall *(ENTER THREE SHEPHERDS)* Oh Gosh, You've come again.?
FIRST SHEPHERD	We had to come right back for on our way, we heard that the king is killing throughout the land.
SECOND SHEPHERD	Every male child who is two years old or under must die at his command.
THIRD SHEPHERD	And So, we have come to warn you folks, please slide out of HEROD'S land.
MARY	This is serious. The Whole world is getting to know what our troubles are. No wonder we are getting news from both near and far. *(A GROUP OF PERSONS ENTER COMPRISING ZACH ARIAS, ELIZABETH, SHAMNA, EPHRAIM, CHARLOTTE, JEPHETH AND RHODA. THEY EMBRACE MARY AS SHE BREAKS INTO A SOB.)* MARY CONTINUES. I do not deserve this. Really. I am not worthy. The joy and the honor is just too much for me alone. *(GROUP ON STAGE SAYS THE BENEDICTUS (ZACHARIAS'S SONG) IN RESPONSE AS A TRIBUTE.)*

Blessed be the Lord, the God of Israel.
He has come to his people and set them free.
He has raised up for us a mighty savior,
born of the house of his servant David.
Through his holy prophets he promised of old
that he would save us from our enemies,
from the hands of all who hate us.
He promised to show mercy to our fathers.
and to remember his holy covenant.

This was the oath he swore to our father Abraham:
to set us free from the hands of our enemies,
free to worship him without fear,
holy and righteous in his sight all the days of
our life.
You, my child, shall be called the prophet of
the Most High.
for you will go before the Lord to prepare his way,
to give his people knowledge of salvation
by the forgiveness of their sins.
In the tender compassion of our God
the dawn from on high shall break upon us,
to shine on those who dwell in darkness and
the shadow of death,
and to guide our feet into the way of peace.
Glory to the Father and to the Son and to the
Holy Spirit,
as it was in the beginning, is now, and will
be forever.

(THEN AN OLD MAN ENTERS WHO IS SIMEON. HE BARGES THROUGH THE CROWD AND IN TURN HE EMBRACES MARY AND JOSEPH.)

JOSEPH	The old man Simeon
MARY	We'll never get to Egypt. Simeon, we'll have to go to Egypt or Herod will kill our son.
SIMEON	I know. I have heard all about it, but you cannot go until I have taken my boy in my arms and look upon his face.
MARY	*(REACHING DOWN FOR THE BABY)* So as The Lord has revealed, I give Him to you. *(SHE GIVES THE BABY TO SIMEON. SIMEON TAKES BABY AND PROCEEDS TO REPEAT THE NUNC DIMMITTIS AS THE CURTAIN SLOWLY CLOSES AS SIMEON REPEATS THE NUNC DIMMITTIS.)*

SIMEON   Lord, now lettest thou thy servant depart in
                                peace according to thy word.
                                For mine eyes have seen thy salvation,
                                Which thou hast prepared before the face of
                                all people.
                                To be a light to lighten the Gentiles and to be
                                the glory of thy people Israel.

(AS CURTAIN REOPENS FOR CURTAIN CALL, MAIN CHARACTERS POSITION THEMSELVES IN SINGING MEDLEY OF CHRISTMAS CAROLS. FINAL CAROL IS "AS WITH GLADNESS MEN OF OLD" ON WHICH CURTAIN CLOSES FOR THE LAST TIME.)

BELIEVE ME I BELIEVE

List of traditional songs and carols included in musical.
These can be found in most traditional church hymnals
or online.

1. Once in Royal David's City

2. Precious Lord, Take My Hand

3. A Virgin Most Pure as the Prophets Do Tell

4. Yes, God Is So Good in Earth and Sky

5. Away in a Manger

6. Thou Didst Leave Thy Throne and Thy Kingly Crown

7. Hark the Herald Angels Sing

8. Angels We Have Heard on High

9. Come Thou Long Expected Jesus

10. While Shepherds Watched Their Flocks by Night

11. O Come All Ye Faithful

We're Not Alone

Text: ERROL LESLIE

Music: ERROL LESLIE

The Christmas Story

LYRICS: ERROL LESLIE

MUSIC: ERROL LESLIE

sto - ry is a - bout the Lord Je - sus Christ; He's the ba - by that was born In a man - ger
dark and dirt - y that first Christ - mas morn He came in - to the world, to make us clean and
feel for - ev - er wor - thy___ For now, in our lives, we have Je - sus Christ We give thanks to
God; we re - joice and are glad That the Fa - ther sent Him to save us___
___ So, lift up your hands, give thanks to our heav - en - ly dad___

Don't Leave Me Guardian Angel

Text: ERROL LESLIE

Music: ERROL LESLIE

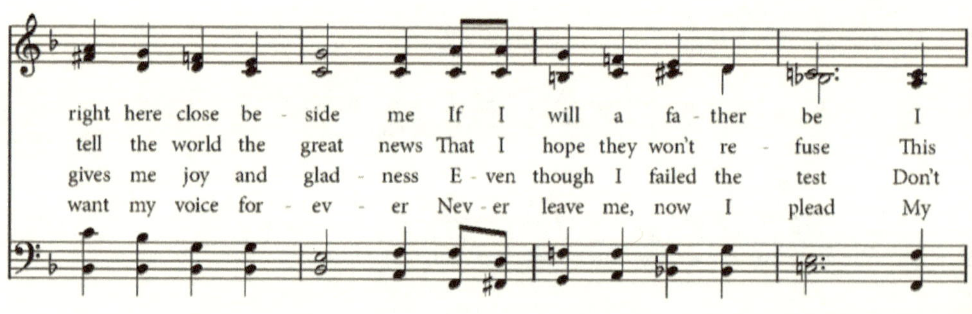

Good News, Bad News

Text: ERROL LESLIE

Music: ERROL LESLIE

An Angel Came to Me

Text: ERROL LESLIE

Music: ERROL LESLIE

An Angel Came to Me

God of Our Fathers

MUSIC: TRADITIONAL
ARRANGEMENT: ERROL LESLIE

Herod's Song

LYRICS: ERROL LESLIE

MUSIC: ERROL LESLIE

ABOUT THE AUTHOR

The Rev. Dr. Errol E Leslie is the founding pastor of Grace and Mercy Ministries Inc. Palm Bay, Florida. Prior to starting that congregation, he served as a pastor in the Methodist Church of the Caribbean and the Americas, as well as the Florida and the New England Conferences of the United Methodist Church.

He is originally from Jamaica where he attended high school, college, and seminary. In high school, he was very involved in the interschool Christian fellowships and participated in several weekend residential camps, all of which turned out to be spiritually uplifting.

After graduating seminary, he served a number of small churches where he specialized in evangelism and youth ministry to include being a camp counsellor for several years in the Methodist church.

He previously published the book Stolen Grace in which he tells the story of his journey in and departure from the United Methodist Church.

Although not having any professional training in theater, Rev. Dr. Leslie has used his innate talent throughout the years to utilize drama as a very useful and effective tool throughout his ministry.

His love for and involvement in drama started from his days in high school when he would work backstage during productions as well as playing various roles onstage including several lead roles. During this same period as a teenager, he would write, direct, and produce Christian plays which were done competitively at church events. He also wrote plays which did not necessarily carry a Christian theme, but still earned rave reviews in the communities in which they would be performed.

His passion for the arts continued during his college and seminary days as once more, he would play leading roles in plays at that level. His first opportunity to perform internationally came in 1976 when he visited Nassau in the Bahamas for a series of concerts. He then participated in both drama and music as he was also a member of the UTCWI (United Theological College of the West Indies) singers.

Rev. Dr. Leslie is also a singer and a self-taught musician with the gift of being able to play several musical instruments. For a long time, he and his family participated in a reggae gospel music ministry where they were able to minster in song to several audiences all over Jamaica and in several states within the USA.

He is happy to share these two musicals with the rest of the world, with the hope that there will be several more Bible-based musicals to follow.

www.ingramcontent.com/pod-product-compliance
Lightning Source LLC
Chambersburg PA
CBHW022011150726
47990CB00002B/612